Beyond the Box

Beyond the Box

Mission Challenges from John's Gospel

Tom Stuckey

British Library Cataloguing in Publication data

A catalogue record for this book is available
from the British Library

ISBN 1 85852 285 4

First published 2005
Reprinted 2006

First published by Inspire
4 John Wesley Road
Werrington
Peterborough PE4 6ZP

Printed and bound in Great Britain by
Arrowsmith, Bristol

In memory of Father Michael who
was murdered in a far country

Preface

When I began this book I was asking myself where God might be leading me in the next phase of my own theological and spiritual journey. That question was answered when at the 2004 Methodist Conference in Loughborough I was unexpectedly designated President of the Methodist Conference for the year 2005 to 2006. I now know something of what lies before me though the magnitude of the challenge does somewhat overwhelm me. This book will serve as an important resource as I travel around the country attempting to remind people of the importance of mission, theological reflection and responding to the Spirit.

A number of people are named in the stories included here. In some cases I have altered the names and slightly changed the narrative so that persons and locations cannot be identified. Other names and examples have not been meddled with and I wish to acknowledge those who have provided material: Revd Ralph Ward (p. 24), Revd Tony Morling (p. 26), Mrs Sue Gowling (p. 40), Revd Keith Town (p. 54) and Ms Constance Gooding (p. 57).

Many have helped in writing and bringing this manuscript to publication. I am particularly grateful to Revd Professor David Catchpole for reading the script and as a New Testament scholar bringing a constructive critique to my use of John's Gospel. I have only been able to accommodate some of his suggestions and so recognize that my interpretation of the Gospel remains open to challenge. Revd Peter McNeill not only keeps my computer going but has read the script and helped to make it more accessible for the person in the pew. Thanks are again due to Revd Eric Renouf for commenting on the various drafts and checking the biblical references. I wish to place on record my thanks to Mrs Marilyn Pack, my PA and District Administrator, who for the last seven years has made sure that my diary is sensibly organized, so giving me time to think and write! I also thank Inspire and Dr Natalie K. Watson for their willingness to publish what I have written.

As President I wanted to make sure that my book challenged but did not create too many unhelpful waves for members of the Methodist Connexional Team. They do invaluable work and I record my appreciation of their support. Revd David Deeks, the General Secretary of the Methodist Church, has kindly commented on the text and framed many of the questions for which I am most grateful.

My family needs special mention: Martin, my son (p. 104), Bronwen, my daughter-in-law, my two grandchildren, Ben and Sam; Matthew, my other son, and my daughter, Joanne. I dedicate what I have written to them. My final dedication must of course be to my wife, Christine, who is mentioned on pages 29 and 103. Having already put up with me when, on days off or in the middle of the night, I disappeared into the study to write my previous book, I have done the same thing again. Thankfully this time around, I have managed to contain the process within 14 months. Chris has both encouraged me and been involved in reading the material. This has given me the extra incentive to complete the task quickly. I promise you, Chris, I will not be writing another book for a while.

Contents

1

Visiting the cathedral

'I'm fed up with the church, it is so boring.' I had to agree with her. This 13-year-old had stayed for much longer than I had expected. In the last few months her attendance and that of her friend had been very sporadic. Life outside the church was much more interesting.

He came home from the church meeting exasperated and said to his wife, 'I don't think I will go again.' Martin has a responsible job in London. He had arrived home from work at 7.30, and spent a few minutes with his young son before rushing out to a meeting. There had been no time to talk or eat. The church meeting finished at 10.45. The minister had no idea how to chair it and nearly an hour was spent talking about the flower rota. Martin had so much to give but the meeting was preoccupied with trivialities.

These two stories tell us that the institutional Church is in big trouble. Its relentless decline seems unstoppable. Few predict an upturn. Ministers and leaders of traditional churches spend much of their time talking about money and devising strategies to keep the institution afloat. While the world rushes by like a river in flood, nice people spend hours debating whether to take out a few pews. It is hardly surprising that disillusioned members drop out or move off to one of the newer churches. It is not the first time that great swathes of churches have been wiped out or replaced by something else. God is always passing judgement on churches and attempting to reform them. I believe God is punching holes in the institution because he wants to reshape it. He is calling us to plant new seeds of church alongside the old since much of the old, in its resistance to change, will not survive. This is no simple reshuffling of the pack but rather a call to play a different game, one requiring courage and theological ability. We can no longer keep doing more of the same. We have to live beyond the box.

Out of the box

How do we break out of theological and ecclesiastical boxes? Where do we look for clues? Church history is full of examples of theological shifts, reformations and revivals as God through his Spirit has created fresh expressions of church. Nevertheless, looking to the past has its dangers. There is the temptation to lift out some nostalgic moment and through prayer and faith claim that God 'will do it again'. It is never that simple. God is a living God who makes all things new. Our current culture tempts us to go for simple solutions by abandoning theology and ignoring the wisdom of the past. This too is a dead end. I am persuaded that if we are to engage effectively with contemporary society we must at the same time enter into a critical dialogue with our foundational documents. This raises the question of which bit of the Christian tradition we latch on to. It is often an arbitrary decision. I am going to draw from John's Gospel because it gives me a number of clues about how God might be reshaping today's Church.

Isn't it presumptuous of someone who is not a New Testament scholar to write about John's Gospel? It certainly is! I once entered a vast supermarket and stood bewildered by the display of foodstuffs. I had gone in to buy something simple for tea. Completely overwhelmed I gave up, left and purchased fish and chips on the way home. It was quicker. A lot of people have written a lot of books about John's Gospel.[1] From the stacked volumes of commentaries, theologies, expositions and meditations, which book does the ordinary church member choose? I have written this book for those who want a fast food version. This excursion into John therefore carries a scholarly health warning since it has some flaws and limitations.

In my previous book on mission entitled *Into the Far Country*, I adopted a traditional theological way of writing as I sought to reinterpret the 'great commission' of Matthew 28.18-20.[2] Drawing on theological material and experiences from the non-western world I sought to provoke new thinking at home. Some readers of that book have encouraged me to unpack the ideas, restate, simplify and develop them further. I have tried, therefore, to be more practical and through example and story show how such insights relate to our own situation.

While Mark begins his Gospel with the Baptist, Matthew with Abraham, and Luke with Adam, John reaches back even further and sets his account beyond time, placing the Church's story beyond the box. I therefore invite you to accompany me on a journey of exploration into and beyond John. We shall be looking at how the Gospel seeks to make a connection between our world and John's world.

A wonderful cathedral

I often worship in Winchester Cathedral. There is something timeless about such an impressive building. Yet for all its ancient splendour it is a patchwork of styles with its Norman transepts and Gothic nave. One surveys an evolving history reflecting the ingenuity of nameless builders, masons, labourers and craftsmen. So, too, this monumental Gospel of John. It is one of the baffling books of the New Testament and yet one of the most profound. Like Winchester Cathedral, in which a later architectural design is added on to an earlier one, some scholars suggest that there were two stages in this Gospel production. There was a relatively short first edition. New material was then superimposed to produce the longer second edition which we have today. This would account for the various dislocations which scholars detect in the text.

The four gospels are like four different cathedrals. They all witness to the glory of God and the good news of Jesus Christ, yet they have their own unique structure, character and style. In the magnificence of a cathedral it is not easy discovering the human Jesus. So too with the gospels. Jesus remains an enigmatic figure hidden behind ecclesiastical presentation. John's Gospel is therefore all the more puzzling as the writer appears to offer an intimate picture of Jesus by concentrating on just a few episodes in his life, giving us scenes not found in the other gospels, and by recording long scripted conversations which Jesus is supposed to have had with Nicodemus, the woman at the well, the Pharisees, the disciples in the upper room, and Pilate the governor.

I am going to introduce you to John's Gospel as if I were taking you on a tour of a cathedral. I invite you to enter, mindful of the complexity of its formation yet at the same time ask you not to be distracted by it. Although I will give you bits of information as we go along, I will not be your tour guide. I want you to catch the glory of the place, sense the mystery and be transfigured by it. Above all I want you to meet the Living God. If this happens, your ideas about evangelism and church will not only shift and grow but, more importantly, so too will your under-standing of God. My hope is that, like Thomas the disciple, words of confession will similarly bubble up from your soul, 'My Lord and my God!'(20.28).

We begin by standing outside the cathedral. From some vantage point we contemplate the full vista of this gospel witness to God. At Salisbury the spire points us to the beyond. At Wells the west front, alive with figures of bishops, saints and apostles, transports us upwards to the eternal Father. The prologue of John's Gospel offers us a similar perspective of eternity (1.1-18) and invites us to 'come and see' (1.39). We enter the nave but before proceeding down its length pause at the font. We think of John the Baptist (1.23-34), water turned into wine (2.1-11), the woman at the well (4.7-15) and the healing pool of Bethesda (5.1-9). In the nave are six great arches which heighten the drama and build up our expectation. These arches or 'signs', as John prefers to call them, are the astonishing actions of Jesus which provoke discussion and debate.[3] Within this cathedral Jesus Christ is unveiled as the great I AM.[4] We are now ready to enter the chancel and choir. New intimacies await us as we are washed clean and prepared (13.1-17). In this holy place (chapters 14-17) is the altar of our Lord's high-priestly prayer. No longer observers, we become participants in his glory as the story moves into passion and resurrection (chapters 18-21).

It is time to depart but before doing so we should visit the Lady chapel. As we shall see, the female presence is very strong in this Gospel. Returning by the side aisles we pass the tombs of the great and the good, reminding us of our mortality, while soaring figures of saints speak of resurrection. Before leaving we pause once more to look back down the nave. Shafts of light flood in to dispel darkness. The lofty pillars, like huge tree trunks, and the Gothic tracery on the high ceilings evoke memories of forests. We are inside a cathedral and yet we are contemplating God's good green creation.

The disciple whom Jesus loved

Because the New Testament documents appeared in a haphazard way scholars continue to debate their sources and the places of origin. I am going to assume that John's Gospel was written in Ephesus. Of course, there are alternatives ranging from Antioch, Syria, and the Golan Heights, to Alexandria in Egypt. The greater puzzle surrounds the actual writing of the Gospel.

Appearing enigmatically is someone described as 'the disciple whom Jesus loved'.[5] We do not know his name. There have been a number of suggestions. The traditional answer is John, the unnamed companion of Andrew, who makes his entry in the opening chapter (1.40). He is also the one who stands at the foot of the cross with Mary the mother of Jesus and becomes her adopted son. Another candidate is Lazarus who is named as the object of Jesus' love. Another possibility is the secret disciple who knew the high priest and let Peter into his house (18.15). A further contender is Nathanael. He is the 'true Israelite' like Jacob of old. He confesses Jesus to be the Son of God and the King of Israel (1.47-51). Moreover, his home town is Cana in Galilee, a familiar location in John's Gospel.

This 'beloved disciple' became a man of authority and influence within the Ephesian church. He was a source of many of the stories and sayings of Jesus. He had personally been with the first disciples and witnessed some of the main events of Jesus' life. In Ephesus, young Christians must have hung on his words and drew on his wisdom. It is reported that he lived to a ripe old age, revered by a new generation of Christians. When finally the old man died at the age of 100 it became even more important to gather up and preserve the true stories, sayings and traditions which had become so profuse (21.25).

There had been a rumour that the 'beloved disciple' would still be around when Jesus Christ returned on the clouds of glory (21.23). His death must have come as a great shock to the church. Was this the incentive which led to the creation of John's Gospel? Many in Ephesus would have been familiar with the Gospels of Matthew, Mark and Luke so there was a big job to be done. We do not know the names of the editors and writers who gathered up, sifted the material and shaped it through several editions into the Gospel we have now. For convenience sake throughout this book I will refer to them as 'the writers' of John's Gospel. This Gospel indeed resembles a cathedral on which many imaginative people have worked.

Vision and reality

While this was going on in Ephesus, other New Testament churches were developing their own structures, patterns of ministry, statements of faith, and celebrating the sacraments of baptism and Eucharist. Peter and the 12 apostles, including Paul, were dominant figures in the treasured memory of the Church. This memory is preserved and idealized in the Acts of the Apostles.

The writers of John's Gospel, aware of these developments, set out to write an alternative gospel reminding the Christian community of the time before the apostles. They root their gospel in Jesus himself. Put crudely, they prefer the house-group to the cathedral. There is no mention of special apostles or church order. All Christians are followers of Jesus and described as disciples. Indeed, Peter, who had been given high status in many churches, was downgraded. Five hundred disciples witnessed the resurrection, so Peter was just one of the many heroes and heroines who followed Jesus from the beginning. The writers' ideal was not the fast-growing apostolic Church but the earlier Christian community meeting in Jerusalem after the ascension, made up of ordinary people like Peter, John, James, Andrew, Philip, Thomas, Nathanael (Bartholomew), Matthew, James the son of Alphaeus, Simon the Zealot, Judas the son of James, the women (presumably Mary the wife of Clopas, Mary Magdalene, Martha), Mary the mother of Jesus and her other sons including James plus about 150 others (Acts 1.13-15).

There is irony in the fact that the writers, in proposing an intimate and almost sect-like pattern of church, end up constructing a cathedral-like gospel. Ecclesiastical life is never straightforward. The church in Ephesus was to be torn apart by faction and heresy. Paul had predicted this:

> Keep watch over yourselves and over all the flock, of which the Holy Spirit has made you overseers [bishops?] ... I know that after I have gone, savage wolves will come in among you, not sparing the flock. Some even from your own group will come distorting the truth in order to entice the disciples to follow them. Therefore be alert ... (Acts 20.28-31)

These wolves were obviously prowling around when the writers paint their portrait of the Good Shepherd (10.1-17). In the New Testament we also have three letters ascribed to John which seem to reflect this troubled situation. I hazard a guess that they may have been penned by other unknown writers who also once sat at the feet of the 'beloved disciple'. The story does not end here. Another of these, one of 'their brothers and companions', produced a pamphlet from his island prison on Patmos (Revelation 1.9). Churches in Asia were suffering from a vicious persecution. These visions, given under the inspiration of the Holy Spirit, sought to stoke up the courage of Christians by enabling them to see contemporary events within the time-frame of God's eternal providence. As in the prologue of John's Gospel they are reminded of a Christ who was there at the beginning and will be there at the end. Yet the spiritual health of the Ephesian church is still suspect:

> I know your works, your toil and your patient endurance. I know that you cannot tolerate evildoers; you have tested those who claim to be apostles but are not, and have found them to be false ... But I have this against you, that you have abandoned the love you had at first. Remember then from what you have fallen; repent, and do the works you did at first. (Revelation 2.2-5)

In spite of these troubles, churches were growing rapidly as Christians sought to flood the Roman Empire with the Father's glory. At the points of interface where the message had radically penetrated the Hellenistic (Greek/Roman) culture, important theological and ethical questions had arisen. Should the Church wage war on everything in the prevailing culture or should it adopt parts of that culture? If the latter, how much of the culture should it absorb? Such questions have always been with us and never more so than now. Western Christians live today in a culture saturated with consumerism, fundament-alisms, and a rampant individualism which is destroying all notions of the common good. To what extent has our understanding of the gospel been distorted by these powerful forces? When the Christian West sent out missionaries to other lands, they were forced to wrestle with the problem of communicating across cultural barriers. Now that mission field is on our doorstep and the Church is viewed by most outsiders as an alien, irrelevant institution. Sometimes I think our contemporary culture has more in common with the first and second centuries than the ecclesiastical world of our grandparents.

Mission challenges

Mission means movement. 'As the Father has sent me,' says the risen Christ, 'I am sending you' (20.21). Embedded in John's Gospel are a number of mission challenges to get us moving beyond the box. Some relate directly to the commands of Jesus, others are implied by his actions or spring out of issues addressed by the writers. A particular challenge will head each of the chapters which follow. So that you can see what's in store I have listed them here.

- Allow God's Spirit to reshape your church, so that it becomes flexible, open, fluid and responsive to God's future rather than stuck in the rut of its own past.

- Allow God's Spirit personally to renew and empower you, so turning you into an active, obedient disciple of Jesus Christ.

- God himself is diversity in unity. He wants his Church to be one yet also to celebrate its diversity. Look beyond your own local church and seek to engage in mission with partners from other churches and with anyone else who is willing to work with you.

- Some of us like to control things while others collude with this. Can we break up existing power bases in order to develop and encourage more creative relationships between different people, giving particular attention to the contribution of the disempowered and those on the margins of society?

- Get stuck into the bigger concerns of social justice. The Church is not meant to be a cosy club but is called to be a prophetic and counter-cultural community.

- Discipleship may demand costly sacrifices. Pray and obey. There is no other way of expressing our love and commitment to Jesus.

- Let's move out of the comfort zone. We and our churches must wrestle with deeper issues and begin to talk to outsiders about God, so that they too can become disciples of Christ.

- Let's remain open to God and keep moving on with him. There is life in abundance if we move beyond the box.

Just visiting

How are you going to visit this cathedral of John's Gospel? Will it be a whistle-stop tour allowing you to rush in and out, just to say that you have been? Will you do the set tour, following your guide around as she tells the story, stopping from time to time to draw your attention to some intricate detail you have missed? When your visit is over and you stand at the exit, will you pause and take stock or rush off to the cathedral restaurant to get a cup of tea and a cream cake?

To help you think about the challenges arising from your visit, I have put questions at the end of each chapter. You may wish to look at these on your own or discuss them with others. This book can be used both for personal reflection and also for group study. Some of you may find it helpful to look at the questions before reading the chapters. They, like the challenges, will give you some indication of the content of the chapter.

You will also see that prayers are included after the questions. In these I sometimes use 'I' and sometimes 'we'. All prayer is corporate even when you pray on your own. I hope you will feel able to use these prayers both in your private devotions and when you meet as a group. Studying the Bible and thinking about God's call to mission should always be done prayerfully.

In entering John's Gospel I hope this book will be your guide book, but your real guide has to be the Holy Spirit. The Spirit will take you around and open your eyes to the wonders of the place. I want you to stop and stare. I want you to sit and let the glory of John's written cathedral seep into your soul. I want you to sense the secret presence of the living God, the great I AM who invites you to worship and adore. If this happens you will not be aware of the exit, for even when you pass outside, the cathedral experience will linger and remain with you and in you. Thus every future encounter will be touched with the divine, and every common place will become holy ground.

QUESTIONS

1. How are you going to read and handle these questions? On your own? In a group?

2. Take time to read the Gospel through as you would any other booklet, from beginning to end. Use a good modern translation like the *New Revised Standard Version* (which is quoted throughout this book) or the *New International Version*, or a version in the contemporary idiom like *The Message* (very accessible). [This is good preparation for looking in detail at the particular passages you will encounter in this book.]

3. The contemporary Church is in big trouble. What do you think God is trying to say to us? What is your initial response to the mission challenges listed in this chapter?

PRAYER

Father God, help me to read John's Gospel with
    fresh anticipation
        and a clear determination to discover its
            hidden secrets.
May your Holy Spirit be my guide,
    may Jesus be my way,
        may the 'beloved disciple' be my inspiration.
            Open my heart and mind to your truth
                and your life.

Amen

2

Shrines and vines

Allow God's Spirit to reshape your church, so that it becomes flexible, open, fluid and responsive to God's future rather than stuck in the rut of its own past.

I enter this vast Victorian edifice of crumbling splendour. I remember the damp walls, peeling plaster, wheezing organ and boxed pews with doors to protect the congregation from draughts, outsiders and change. I also recall the dismal ancillary buildings, with their decaying halls linked by narrow uneven passages with steps designed to trip the unwary. When I was last here in this cavernous 900-seat auditorium three years before, 22 people hid themselves at the back in the gloom beneath the balcony. The new minister to be welcomed on this occasion wondered if his frail congregation would outlast the service if it went on for too long. This time, however, there were visitors from other churches who had come to view the novelty of a young minister. I was uplifted by the sight of two beautiful floral displays lovingly arranged by some friend of the congregation. Their glory contrasted sharply with the ecclesiastical glory which had clearly departed. I preached on John 2.12-22, the cleansing of the temple. As I spoke on the words, 'Destroy this temple and I will raise it again in three days', I found myself thinking about another saying of Jesus, 'Your house is left to you desolate' (Luke 13.35, NIV). This exhausted building was a sad reminder that over the past 20 years there had been a number of opportunities for change and redevelopment. Tragically the controlling elite had resisted all.

Temples, old and new

> Jesus went up to Jerusalem. In the
> temple he found people selling cattle,
> sheep, and doves, and the money-
> changers seated at their tables. Making a
> whip of cords, he drove all of them out of
> the temple, both the sheep and cattle. He
> also poured out the coins of the money-
> changers and overturned their tables. He
> told those who were selling the doves,
> 'Take these things out of here! Stop
> making my Father's house a market-
> place!'... The Jews then said to him,
> 'What sign can you show us for doing
> this?' Jesus answered them, 'Destroy this
> temple, and in three days I will raise it
> up.' The Jews then said, 'This temple has
> been under construction for forty-six
> years, and you will raise it up in three
> days?' But he was speaking of the temple
> of his body. After he was raised from the
> dead, his disciples remembered that he
> had said this. (2.13-21)

Jesus uses two devastating words to describe the
Jerusalem temple which outsiders might repeat from
their own experience of the institutional Church. The
house is 'desolate' and it has become a 'market'.

As attendance figures continue to decline, many of
our church buildings have become houses of
desolation. The form of worship often reflects the
nostalgic childhood religion of the attendees who
appear reluctant to give up their choirs, pews and
'children's address'. Some ministers and preachers
collude with this. The ebbing tide of churchgoing in
the West is in marked contrast to what is happening
in other parts of the world. In Europe and North
America we are haemorrhaging members at a rate of

7,600 per day while Africa alone is making 16,400 new Christians daily. Where nearly empty church buildings in towns and villages glower at each other within a stone's throw, church leaders look for an ecumenical answer to make more effective use of diminishing resources. Their solution is fewer and more strategically placed church buildings. Sadly, this is often resisted by local people nostalgically attached to their shrine.

The Jerusalem temple of John's Gospel was not a place of desolation. It bubbled with life. Its courts were thronged with the hustle and bustle of thousands of people and its worship area was drenched in praise. While some churches are places of desolation others pulsate with activity. Vibrancy in today's church is often measured by the quantity of activities appearing on the notice sheet, the flow of outsiders through its premises during the week and the number and age of worshippers on Sunday. Playgroups, coffee mornings, Scouts, Brownies, fellowship meetings, lunch clubs, badminton, youth groups, house-groups, Alpha groups, Bible studies; surely these signify that the church is alive? To facilitate this, buildings are modernized and made more welcoming. This helps to increase the regular congregation by drawing outsiders in. Lights blaze out at night from every room. Surplus space is hired out for community service. This also generates money to run the whole enterprise. Like a buzzing bee-hive the building hums with activity. But is worship, prayer and praise, as in the old Jewish temple, always the spiritual focus and hub for these activities?

Like products on the supermarket shelves the different brands of worship offer a wide variety of choice, from noisy 'all-age worship', swinging charismatic exuberance, all the way across to the echoing other-worldly chants of the cathedral choir or the Quaker silence. In our age of mobility younger Christians shop around for a church package which suits their current spiritual needs. What appears as growth in one church precipitates fall in another in an overall statistic of decline. In a fast moving world, denomination, location and tradition are no longer as important as they were for the older generation of churchgoers. Attending church can resemble other leisure-time activities like the golf club or a regular spell at the gym. In Britain Sunday churchgoing is being replaced by the utilitarian conviviality of the car-boot sale. The bright shopping malls in our cities are becoming the contemporary cathedrals, celebrating the triumph of consumerism. However we look at it, 'the glory has departed'. Keeping the Church going has become a displacement activity papering over the spiritual void at the heart of established western Christianity. The church building may be a house of prayer, it can also resemble a market-place trading spiritual wares.

While today's Church may suffer from some of the same maladies as the Jewish temple of Jesus' time, it does not entirely fulfil the same purpose nor does it act as its modern substitute. The large General Hospital fulfils that role. Like an anthill the hospital heaves with activity but, unlike the institutional Church or the shopping mall, it deals directly with issues of life, death, trauma and pain. It is a place of cut flesh and gushing blood. Its primary task is to deliver healing and cure by ameliorating pain and distress. Here, serious conversations about ultimate things take place, but here too money, budgets and numbers set limits to the amount of healing on offer. The high priests are no longer the doctors and surgeons but the multitude of managers who oversee this vast contemporary temple. Nevertheless, just as the General Hospital relates to the local health centres, so the Jerusalem temple related to the synagogues which energized worship in people's homes. The worshipping focus of Judaism was to pass beyond the temple, to the synagogue, to the home and even to the prison cells of Auschwitz. The Jews were to learn how to live as a dispersed people without a temple and often with no religious building at all. Ironically the Church was to evolve in a contrary direction and create replacement temples to house the things of God.

Shrines and signs

The temple built by Solomon must have been magnificent. It had the reputation of being one of the seven wonders of the ancient world. It drew people from far away, fulfilling Israel's religious dream of being the focal point of God's worship on earth (Isaiah 2.1-4). It became the symbol of kingly power and national pride. During the time of the prophet Isaiah it acquired an almost magical significance so that many Jews started to believe Jerusalem to be inviolable. The prophet Jeremiah thought otherwise. Unfortunately the city lay in the path of marching armies. The superpowers of the ancient world, Assyria, Babylon, Persia, Greece and Rome, were to trample through it. When the first temple was destroyed by Nebuchadnezzar in 587 BC much of its glory had already been ripped away to buy off the conquerors who menaced the land. The replacement temple, built some 70 years later, was but a shadow of Solomon's wondrous construction. In addition the post-exilic cosmopolitan population of Jerusalem posed problems for people like Nehemiah and his successors who sought to protect the holiness of God. This probably led to the courtyard being partitioned to filter true Jews in, thereby keeping others out. This arrangement was further amplified in King Herod's upgrading of the building in the years preceding Christ's birth.

Some archaeologists think that underneath the Jerusalem temple was a huge storage area like an underground car park. This echoing subterranean vault housed the booths of the money changers, the pungent pens of animals and the traders in spiritual knick-knacks. It was a noisy, smelly, overcrowded, airless place of flaring lamps and belligerent bargaining. One storey above was the official place of prayer and on top was the holy of holies. If this was indeed the architectural design we have a dramatic picture of an institution which on the outside had all the features of uplifting worship but which rested on the cheap-jack wares of the religious con man. One can therefore imagine the panic as Jesus smashes up the stalls and releases flapping pigeons into this confined space.

Not a good way to start

There was a minister called Jim whose story went like this. He arrived in September. In October he introduced some modern songs which the organist refused to play. In November he tried to persuade the robed choir to move from their traditional stalls at the front where most had sat for the last 40 years. In December he suggested that the pews be ripped out and replaced with chairs. In January a music group was formed and the organist stormed out. In February the church council was divided on the issue of derobing the choir. In March the choir master and church secretary resigned. In April an 'all-age worship service' was held, attracting some young families who then started to come. In May a little group plotted to get rid of the minister. In June there was a huge bust-up. In July the minister, his wife and children left and the new young families gave up coming. In September a retired minister of the church took over and things went back to normal. But what is normal?

It is strange that John's Gospel places the cleansing of the temple at the beginning of Jesus' ministry. The other Gospels timetable this angry entry towards the end of his public ministry, setting it in the context of his final verbal shoot-out with the religious authorities. This textual dislocation could be the result of a piece of bad editing by the writers, who also spice up the violence. Nevertheless, this positioning and link with the first miracle in Cana of Galilee, as we shall see, has profound theological significance.

Jesus' action in the temple leaves us in no doubt that his idea of normality is radically different from ours. While Mark and Luke explain it in terms of reform so that 'prayer for all the nations' becomes the focus of temple life (Mark 11.17), John goes further. Just as the old watery religion of Judaism is to be replaced by the new wine of the Spirit so 'the temple building' is to be replaced by 'Jesus the true vine'. From now on in this Gospel, the building ceases to be a place of prayer and turns into an arena for argument and confrontation (7.15; 8.2 and 59). Like old skins the temple can no longer contain the bubbling new wine of the Spirit about to burst out into the world. The temple, like so many church buildings, had become a shrine encapsulating the past. The resurrection body of Jesus Christ is to be a sign anticipating the future.

Liquefying the fruit of the vine

> I am the true vine, and my Father is the
> vine-grower. He removes every branch in
> me that bears no fruit. Every branch that
> bears fruit he prunes to make it bear
> more fruit. You have already been
> cleansed by the word that I have spoken
> to you. Abide in me as I abide in you.
> Just as the branch cannot bear fruit by

itself unless it abides in the vine, neither can you unless you abide in me. I am the vine, you are the branches. Those who abide in me and I in them bear much fruit, because apart from me you can do nothing. Whoever does not abide in me is thrown away like a branch and withers; such branches are gathered, thrown into the fire, and burned .... My Father is glorified by this, that you bear much fruit and become my disciples. (15.1-6, 8)

Every September, looking out of my study window, I see bunches of grapes beginning to ripen to deep red on the vine attached to our south-facing wall. We have been in this house for seven years, and each year I have become more courageous in my pruning efforts. The harvests have become increasingly fruitful. The image of church as vine is totally organic. The fruitfulness of churches is dependent on their 'abiding' in Christ. This organic model of church places relationships before rules and at the same time minimizes structure and organization. Instead, mutual respect, listening, feeding on the tradition of 'the beloved disciple', devotion to Christ, obedience to his command of love and relying on the Spirit are deemed to be sufficient.

The writers of the Gospel are inviting us to shift from static to liquid models of church. The implications are considerable. The necessity of church buildings, whether desolate or bustling with spiritual market activity, is questioned. Ecclesiastical organizations are to be simplified and democratized. Men and women are to be released from the stranglehold of the institution. Relationships come before rules. Drastic pruning is required to chop out the many displacement activities of local churches since these distort discipleship and rob members of fruitfulness. Oscar Wilde once said that the problem of socialism was that it takes up too many evenings. The same could be said of some churches. The ecclesiastical institution as we have known it probably has a limited shelf-life as it becomes increasingly difficult finding money and volunteers to service the building, organization and structure. Present day churches have to choose between liquefication or liquidation.

Liquid church

In his book, *Liquid Church*, Pete Ward describes two types of church: 'solid church' and 'liquid church'.[1] In his analysis of contemporary society, he argues that western culture is moving to a more fluid form of modernity. He uses the technical word 'modernity' to describe that period in western history where settlement triumphed over impermanence and reason reigned supreme. Technological innovation, he argues, is now occurring at such an alarming rate that change has become the name of the game. Hitherto, modernity has substituted one solid bureaucracy, institution, set of values, or order of relationships for another. Modernity is now undergoing a liquefying process so that everything is becoming flexible, fuzzy and subject to obsolescence. The 'solid church' which once related to solid modernity and pre-modernity is increasingly becoming a diminishing island surrounded by the turbulent seas of change. In some cases these ecclesiastical islands are cold barren places, while others are fairy tale islands inhabited by nice people who want to experience holiday feelings before returning to normal life.

Our liquid culture has undermined time-honoured values of loyalty to place, tradition and denomination. Pete Ward believes ecumenism to be a product of solid modernity. In a liquid culture the multiplicity of churches and denominations are viewed by the public as corner shops offering a range of spiritual goods. He states that 'solid church' has all the features of a heritage site, a refuge and a nostalgic community. He argues that just as the Sunday congregation located in a particular place has been the central pillar of 'solid church', in a postmodern culture mobile networks are essential, and that the fuzzy edges of a particular network are the true growth areas.

I reach a similar conclusion in my book, *Into the Far Country*:

> The diverse tapestry of world-wide ecclesial communities will reflect the rich colours and patterns of the Trinity in whom the many are one and the one many. So churches will not replicate themselves like some multi-national McDonald's. There will be a multiplicity of models of the Church. The institution can no longer be regarded as the primary model. Each church will be different so as to represent some aspect of the multiplicity of languages, peoples and cultures. Their unity will not be the product of ecclesiastical joinery but of the Spirit who baptizes with fire and generates diversity. Each local church, as in the New Testament, will be light in structure, ever ready to respond to its own moment of *kairos*. Partnership links between different ecclesial communities through prayer, shared learning, mutual exchange of members and itinerant ministry, will save them from parochialism and demonstrate catholicity. Thus ecclesial communities will ebb and flow

> to the tides of the Spirit. God is not creating a new set of ecclesiastical institutions but rather a 'fluid' Church reflecting the dancing life of the Trinity, in whom unity and diversity make music together.[2]

Every minister who attempts to introduce change will hit difficulties. The experience of Jim, the minister who lasted a year, is not unique. He certainly moved too fast with a leadership style which antagonized his congregation. Someone said that generals in an army should not get too far ahead of their troops lest they be mistaken for the enemy and shot by their own side. This is what happened to Jim and the newcomers quickly drifted away and went elsewhere. Outsiders with no Christian background are not going to be comfortable in what for them is an alien church culture. 'Solid church' has either to loosen up considerably, which Jim's church refused to do, or we have to establish a different sort of church beyond the box.

Planet X

Planet X has been running for three years in middle school. It started when Ralph shared his vision of an 'alternative church' with a young man who was a DJ in a disco. They went together to the school disco and got to know the staff and young people. Ralph has his own sound equipment so approached the head of the school with a view to running a Christian disco. The head agreed. Ralph gathered his own team of 12 adult helpers and Planet X began. Ralph has all the stage gifts for running the show. It is a kaleidoscope of disco-dancing, games, quiz items, visuals, action songs, PowerPoint® presentations, prayers, chat, tuck, custard pies and fun. Members of the audience are able to come on stage to perform, dance and share in the activities.

There is a post-box for the young people anonymously to list issues they wish to explore. Ralph comments:

> We have dealt with everything from 'how to pray' to 'eating disorders'. It is very demanding on time and energy but we have been drawing audiences of 200 plus since it began. Planet X is being run in four different locations, each drawing similar numbers.

The purpose of the gigs is very clear:

> It is about sharing the love of Jesus; it is a method of evangelism aimed at the 9-13-year-olds who have little or no contact with the Church; it is a way of training teams of evangelists by giving them a vision and showing them how to enact that vision.

There have been all sorts of spin-offs as parents as well as the young people have become interested in Christianity. The question now arises, can we or should we introduce these new 'liquid Christians' into traditional 'solid church'?

Parallel church

For some years I have been advocating the setting up of 'parallel churches'. We may already have some on our church premises, like the mid-week shoppers' service and the women's fellowship attracting people who do not normally come on Sundays. In recent years more radical examples have sprung up in schools, homes, offices and community centres offering a variety of shapes and patterns of fellowship. Some ministers like Jim, frustrated by resistance to change in the local church, are now being released to pioneer 'fresh expressions of church'. Such initiatives should be encouraged since they are not simply alternatives to 'normal' church but may be the green shoots of 'future church'. Many churches are in trouble because God's Spirit is bypassing them since they have become temple shrines for an in-group. I firmly believe that God is calling us to explore new ways of being church. 'Parallel churches' could replace many if not most of our traditional churches.

A new church?

It didn't feel like church or look like church. As I sat at one of the tables waiting for the others to arrive, Brian joined me. We talked about MG sports cars, the stock market, the Iraq war, the Pope, and the inevitable question about what ministers do. He last attended church when he was best man at his brother's wedding. He couldn't remember entering a church before. Although he had never previously spoken to a minister and kept apologizing for his language we ended up exploring profound theological questions of vocation and existence. He had popped in to see the café owner, but stayed on for an hour to talk with me. This was my first experience of Cafe Paris, the brainchild of a minister who sought to create a 'parallel church' attracting those 20-30-year-olds who were either on the edge of 'solid church' or who had little church contact. The idea was simple. Hire a restaurant which offers good food and drink at a reasonable price; invite a friend; come and listen to someone who will speak enthusiastically about God. On this occasion I was the speaker. The event started at 7.30 and we drifted away at 10.45 when the owner closed up. Tony, who had set up this 'parallel church', was also the minister of a thriving established church. This 'liquid church' was a halfway house for outsiders who wished to 'come and see'. Tony reflects:

You can tell something important is happening when the owner and the cooks drift from the kitchen and stand around listening as they polish glasses which are already clean.

I came away thrilled. I had engaged in more conversations about God on that one evening than I generally do in a month of normal church. Whether this 'fresh expression of church' will survive or evaporate is unimportant. It was enough that it happened and Jesus was there.

I now see why the Gospel writer joins up the wedding feast of Cana with our Lord's visit to the temple. The old watery religion has to give way to something new – a gathering of people where the wine of the Spirit flows and where food and laughter break down the barriers of estrangement.

QUESTIONS

1. How does your building help and hinder the mission of God? Make two lists and discuss them.

2. Why do some Christians resist change? What can be done about it?

3. What plans does your church have for developing a fresh expression of church?

   a) What type/group of people do you wish to communicate with?

   b) Where should you meet?

   c) How do you propose going about it?

   d) Do you have persons with the necessary gifts to pioneer a fresh expression of church?

PRAYER

Lord Jesus Christ,

we invite you to enter our church building

   and pass judgement upon all we do.

Grant us discernment to see what prevents outsiders

   from joining our church

      and discovering your risen presence.

Grant us courage to terminate all those traditional activities

   which close us and others off

      from your future.

Grant us faith to loosen up, let go

   and open ourselves up

      so that our church truly becomes your church.

         Through Jesus Christ our Lord.

                                        Amen

3

The breaking of the waters

Allow God's Spirit personally to renew and empower you, so turning you into an active, obedient disciple of Jesus Christ.

It was a rush to get to the small cottage hospital on the outskirts of Bristol. The contractions had started an hour before and the waters had broken. It was the first time I had been present at the birth of one of our children. I was quite good at doing the breathing exercises but that did not help Christine. My enthusiasm for giving her the gas and air mask made her feel so drowsy that she did not want to push. I shall never forget the moment when this wonderful miracle of life emerged into the light and took her first breath. We had a beautiful daughter.

I once led a Bible study with a group of doctors, nurses and midwives on the first four chapters of John's Gospel. It was an illuminating moment when one remarked that the text was all about 'the breaking of the waters' and 'birthing'. I had never seen this before. The symbol of water links it all together; the baptism of Jesus in chapter 1, the turning of water into wine in chapter 2, the demand that Nicodemus be 'born of water and the spirit' in chapter 3 and the story of the woman at the well in chapter 4. These passages are not only damp, they are drenched in 'living water'.

Birthing

The breaking of waters at birth opens up the possibilities of a new life to be lived. The ministry of John the Baptist was the launching pad for Christian discipleship. It was gossiped that Jesus himself baptized but the Gospel writer appears to squash this rumour (4.1-2). Nevertheless it soon became apparent that Jesus was also in the new creation business where waters break and the Spirit flows.

> In the beginning was the Word, and the Word was with God, and the Word was God. He was in the beginning with God. All things came into being through him, and without him not one thing came into being. What has come into being in him was life, and the life was the light of all people. The light shines in the darkness, and the darkness did not overcome it. There was a man sent from God, whose name was John. He came as a witness to testify to the light, so that all might believe through him. He himself was not the light, but he came to testify to the light. The true light, which enlightens everyone, was coming into the world. But to all who received him, who believed in his name, he gave power to become children of God, who were born, not of blood or of the will of the flesh or of the will of man, but of God. (1.1-9, 12-13)

This grand prologue reminds us of the opening verses of the Old Testament. There is darkness; but God pre-exists the darkness. God, the source of light and life, creates through his Word:

> In the beginning when God created the heavens and earth, the earth was a formless void and darkness covered the

face of the deep, while a wind from God
swept over the face of the waters. Then
God said, 'Let there be light'; and there
was light. And God saw that the light was
good; and God separated the light from
the darkness. (Genesis 1.1-4)

The Spirit of God hovers over a primal mess of
chaos. God speaks and the waters break open. He
again utters his Word and light pierces the darkness.
A space is opened up to provide a cosmic stage upon
which God will continue to create. Nothing can
extinguish this light. It blazes away giving birth to all
things, creating and recreating in abandoned
abundance. It permeates and illuminates every
creature on earth.

I have quoted only some of the prologue. You
might want to look up the passage and continue
reading. It rolls on with majestic splendour
describing how the Word finally becomes tangible in
flesh so that all can behold the life, the light, the
glory, the grace and the truth of the Father. Yet
whenever I read the prologue I puzzle, as New
Testament scholars have done, over why this
unfolding cosmic drama is interrupted by the figure
of John the Baptist (1.6-8). He appears on the
platform like some blundering stage-hand in the
opening minutes of the play. Scholars quite rightly
see this as evidence of later writers inserting material
into an earlier version of the Gospel. The result is
clumsy but revealing. In the breaking of the waters
and the birthing of the Word John has a role to play.
He acts as the midwife. He is the voice who delivers
the Word. He helps to present the Son of God to the
waiting crowds. 'Here is the Lamb of God who takes
away the sin of the world!' (1.29).

Water, when accompanied by the words of Jesus
(6.63), takes on sacramental significance. Water,

when not so endowed, is chaotic and dangerous. It, like the tsunami, can drown us for it belongs to what is described as the world of 'the flesh' or 'night'. It has to be subdued and walked upon (6.19). Sacramental water, in contrast, is a gift from the Father (7.37). It wells up, sparkles, is living and life-giving. 'Solid church' becomes a 'liquid church' when the Word speaks, the waters break and the Spirit comes.

The Greek word for 'spirit' is *'pneuma'*, which can be translated as 'wind' or 'breath'. Jesus describes the birthing process to Nicodemus in terms of 'water and spirit', where the 'spirit' is the breath of God coming into us (3.8). This birthing of the Word is not a result of sexual intercourse between partners. We do not become children of God through human intention or desire (1.13), nor through our parentage as the Jews believed. Conception takes place through the supernatural penetration of the Holy Spirit. This is something which Nicodemus, a Jew through the accident of natural birth, could not understand. The Spirit descends gently like a dove bequeathing identity (1.32). The breaking of the waters and the coming of light are one and the same in the evangelists' description of this regenerative activity so evocative of the first moments of creation (Genesis 1.1-13).

Light at the end of the tunnel

For Lazarus the tomb is a womb. His coming out into the bright light of day resembles a birthing process. His grave clothes are wrapped around him like an umbilical cord so that he has to be cut loose. But the birthing process can go wrong. The darkness of the womb can become a tomb. Nicodemus comes out of the night to be with Jesus, but Judas leaves Jesus to go out into the dark. It is darkness of terror, despair and the desire for death. When the waters break we can become trapped in the tunnel of the womb or so traumatized by the birthing process that our lives are lived in the land of shadows. The waters of chaos can drown one's identity. Many British ministers interested in counselling did 'clinical theology' courses in the 1970s. Frank Lake, a qualified psychologist, medical doctor and theologian, fascinated us with his diagrams of how pre-natal disturbances can give rise to personality disorders ranging from hysteria and depression to schizoid and paranoid conditions.[1] Life in the darkness of the womb was not as safe as was once thought, for the foetus could be swimming in a sea of troubles. We have always known that the birthing process for both mother and child was fraught with risk but Frank Lake showed us that being pushed around tight corners could drive a baby 'around the bend'. The child's will to live during such traumas can turn into a desperate desire to die. When this little life arrives into a world of brilliant lights, loud voices, is gripped with hands that may suspend it by the feet, slap it, cut the still-pulsating cord and, as so often used to happen, be dumped into a cot nearby, is to nudge the newborn over the edge.

Frank Lake and his colleagues discovered that deep breathing could be the catalyst for primal recapitulation. His therapy enabled sufferers to relive the traumatic journey from the early weeks following conception to birth itself. He maintained that a rebirthing could take place through the breathing in of the Holy Spirit and the healing of memories. For some ministers, Frank Lake's approach took its place alongside the therapies of the neo-Freudian, the Rogerian and the Behaviourist schools. I do not wish to make any comments about its effectiveness or otherwise. What is significant for us is his theological reflection upon the process of rebirthing. His books are laced with insights not only about personality disorders but about spiritual journey. He highlights many of the issues which the writers of John identify in their description of birthing and rebirthing.

Lost in a labyrinth

Living outside the womb is also fraught with danger. We can escape from a tunnel only to find ourselves lost in a labyrinth. This experience is not confined to those who suffer from mental illness. Living, for many today, is as painful as being born. Our western postmodern culture is obsessed with choice. For the marginalized such choices have a bitter cost. They stare with fascination at electrical products in shopping malls which they can obtain today only by mortgaging tomorrow. In previous generations we found our identity in what we made. Often this was done in the company of others who were part of the production process so that identity was shaped through mutual interdependence. Not so today! Our economy is driven by consumerism. I am what I buy. Our desires are continually stimulated so that we become consumers of things we do not need.

It is hardly surprising, therefore, that in such a culture of change and discontinuity the bewildered seek to return to the imagined safety of the womb. A church offering snug comfort and a warm sense of belonging becomes enticingly attractive to people swimming in a 'sea of troubles'. It offers a womb-like haven into which they can regress. That is why so many churchgoers resist change. They have re-entered the womb; they do not wish to be thrust out and born again.

When Jesus visited Jerusalem in chapter 2 of the Gospel, he went directly to the temple, the place of prestige and power. When he again visits Jerusalem in chapter 5 he goes to the local asylum. This is the hideaway for broken people unfit for the temple. These are the disabled and discriminated against.

They suffer from severe mental and physical impairments. Some lie lethargically on the floor. Others meander aimlessly, lost in their own labyrinth of despair. Excavations in Jerusalem have uncovered this asylum with its huge pool. It was revered not by the Jews but by those who had lapsed into pagan superstition. The contrast between temple and pool could not be greater. This is the place for the shunned and the despised; for those who have given up, lost hope or been beaten into the ground. Nevertheless Jesus comes and speaks to a man who has been here for 38 years. Jean Vanier reflects:

> Many people today are overwhelmed by despair – and not only in asylums.
> It is as if they are paralyzed in mind and heart, like this man in this story.
> They do not know where to turn or what to do in front of all the divisions, wars, corruptions, injustices, poverty, hypocrisy and lies of our world.
> They have lost hope.
> Others are paralyzed because they feel unwanted, put aside;
> they are imprisoned in loneliness and anguish.
> Many young people feel they have no place
> in our overly structured and competitive societies.
> They seek to escape through drugs, alcohol, violence and sex.
> We are all in some way blocked by walls of fear and prejudice,
> unable to love and respect others and to share with them.[2]

Jesus says, 'Do you want to get well?' (5.6). This man is so depressed that he has totally shut out other people, even those who might help him. He has become part of the furniture of this dreadful place. Jesus challenges him to be born again. But this is no invitation to pass through the water like Nicodemus, it is instead a challenge to leave the water behind and re-enter the world which he has abandoned. It is time to stand up and live.

Intimacy

The expression 'I AM' on the lips of Jesus is a recurring motif throughout the Gospel. Jesus knows where he has come from and where he is going. He is clear about his own identity. It has been shaped by his relationship with his Father. His use of 'I AM' reminds us of the divine name revealed to Moses when God spoke to him from the burning bush (Exodus 3.13-14). Jesus is identifying himself with this same eternal God. We catch a glimpse of this in the high-priestly prayer:

> After Jesus had spoken these words, he looked up to heaven and said, 'Father, the hour has come; glorify your Son so that the Son may glorify you, since you have given him authority over all people, to give eternal life to all whom you have given him. And this is eternal life, that they may know you, the only true God, and Jesus Christ whom you have sent. I glorified you on earth by finishing the work that you gave me to do. So now, Father, glorify me in your own presence with the glory that I had in your presence before the world existed. (17.1-5)

Such a claim creates consternation in his opponents (8.58-59) and wonder in his disciples (14.5). He disturbs in order to recreate. He wants to draw all people into the same intimate relationship which he has with the Father. Then, like the good shepherd, Jesus can call us by our true name knowing that we will hear his voice (10.3-4).

Nowhere is this more beautifully expressed than in the account of our Lord's resurrection appearance to Mary. She stands outside the tomb; her eyes blinded with tears and her heart breaking with grief. The tomb has been plundered. She fails to realize that the tomb has become a womb. Jesus has been reborn into resurrection freedom. Locked in her own labyrinth of grief she does not believe. When he speaks her name she knows! Yet she must not cling to him or hold him back; to do so will impede both her own development and that of the risen Christ. She has to let go and get on with her own life. This is true for all who emerge from the womb.

A clear imperative

In a tent near the centre of my home village of Kingsbury Episcopi, the sermon reaches its climax. The evangelist has spelt out that we are all sinners and that the wages of sin is death. As a teenager I was disturbed by what was being said. I felt guilty. Since entering my teens I had been searching for something. Was I hearing the answer? Certainly my friend, who had encouraged me to come to this tent meeting had something I lacked. He seemed to know who he was and talked about God as if God were real. Christianity seemed like an exciting adventure into life. The alternative, an eternity in hell, had little appeal. This evangelistic message was not the sort of thing I heard on Sundays at our local Methodist Church which organized good socials but where members seemed mainly interested in perpetuating their chapel culture. Such was my teenage perception. The two testimonies of changed lives, especially the one given by a very attractive teenage girl, were impressive. Was this for me? Would my face shine like the evangelist's? He said anyone could receive it. All you had to do was 'believe on the Lord Jesus Christ and you will be born again'. It was a good offer! But he added 'you have to confess him openly'. This was a problem. 'Do not leave the tent without taking this important step. What would happen to you if returning home tonight you were knocked down and killed?' I had never heard of this happening in our quiet village where only the occasional car or tractor went by. 'Where would you spend eternity?' he said. 'If you want to be saved, as we pray with our eyes closed, raise your hand. I will see you and God will see you.' People must have raised their hands because he kept saying, 'I see you, thank you. Bless you.' I wanted to open my eyes and look. The three people who must have raised their hands in that prayerful moment were afterwards invited to go forward to be prayed over and receive literature. I wanted to put my hand up and indeed on the last evening of the tent mission I did so and experienced the beginnings of a new birth.[3]

The event described above took place a long time ago and was one of a whole series of religious experiences which changed the direction of my life. Jesus says, 'You must be born again' (3.7). This is no add-on to discipleship but rather its foundational ingredient. Without it we lack intimacy with God and a clear sense of Christian identity. It is not, however, meant to be a one-off event sealed up in the past. It heralds an ongoing process of discipleship by allowing the Holy Spirit to reshape us, renewing us for mission. There will be no change from a solid to a liquid church if this is missing. The rebirthing experience turns law into grace, duty into delight and opens our eyes to new perspectives. To those whose feet are washed by Jesus and prepared for mission, the risen Lord appears bestowing peace and breathing out his life-giving Spirit.

> Jesus said to them again, 'Peace be with you. As the Father has sent me, so I send you.' When he had said this, he breathed on them and said to them, 'Receive the Holy Spirit ...' (20.21-22)

Can this happen to us? It can if we read this Gospel of John and open ourselves up to the possibility of again being renewed by the promised Spirit. Clear a space in your busy life for prayer, reflection and meditation. Do not strive or struggle but rest in the certainty that the wind of the Spirit will breathe new life into you; that the rivers of 'living water' will bubble up; that the gentle Spirit will descend like a dove bestowing identity and purpose. The same applies to your church. Remember that God's grace has already touched your life and his Spirit has been at work in you from the beginning. God's gracious actions in the past will bear fruit in your own present and future. As you were once baptized in water, so you will be baptized in the Holy Spirit.

Energy

When the waters break in a rebirthing process we swim in a sacramental sea of possibility just as Peter did when he discovered that the stranger on the shore was Jesus (21.1-11). With the dawning light energy is released. We have already seen (p.9), that members of the Ephesian church were commended for their deeds, their work and their perseverance. They had nevertheless forsaken their 'first love'. Law had become a substitute for grace so that instead of raising the sails and allowing the wind of the Spirit to drive the ecclesiastical ship through the sea, members were wearily bent over the oars. The driving energy had been lost. A prayer in the letter to the Ephesians reminds Christians of the source of their energy:

> Now to him who by the power at work (*energoumenen*) within us is able to accomplish abundantly far more than all we can ask or imagine, to him be glory ... (Ephesians 3. 20-21)

Notice that we get our word 'energy' from the Greek word describing God at work in us. It follows that we lose energy when we become detached from our deep roots in Christ through the Holy Spirit.

While the Church in the western world is declining, it continues to grow at an incredible rate among the poor of the Two-Thirds World. In 1900 there were 10 million African Christians; now there are 400 million. It has been estimated that by 2025 there will be around 2.6 billion Christians of whom 1.8 billion will reside in Africa, Asia and South America. Yet experiences of new birth still happen in our own country. Here is a story from the year 2000:

> Sue tells how she was brought up in East London in poor and difficult circum-stances. Describing her struggles to become a solicitor, her marriage, the death of close family members and three miscarriages she confessed, 'The emotional pain I experienced was so palpable I could almost touch it. It was a time of

profound loss. In order to cope I put all my efforts into working hard at my career, keeping fit and long-distance running. My own inner strength and resilience kept me going as did the love and support of my loved ones. None of my family and friends until this point were Christians. I had no Christian influences in my life.' She and her family then moved to live in a tiny village near Andover. It was a Monday evening and she had been decorating. Something prompted her to walk down into the village. She stopped outside the tiny Methodist Chapel attracted by the singing within. A harvest sale of produce was advertized. She said, 'I don't know why but I walked in just as I was in my paint splattered decorating clothes. An hour and a half later I came out with my arms full of marrows and my heart full of Christ. I went in with nothing and came out with everything.'

She is now training to be a Christian minister. She, like thousands before her, has experienced the breaking of the waters and the new life which comes from God.

QUESTIONS

1. Bring to mind a personal experience which chimes in with what this chapter describes as 'rebirthing' or 'baptism' in the Holy Spirit. (If you are in a group, share your experiences with one another if you feel confident in doing so.)

2. Some long-serving church members and ministers have lost their energy and enthusiasm for God. Why do you think this has happened?

3. What sort of changes in your local church, or your house-group, would encourage the expectation and the renewal of such experiences as described in this chapter? How would you go about sharing such experience with others in your church so that they too would want to catch an enthusiasm for God?

PRAYER

Lord, something has gone wrong in my life.
> I have become dull, no longer sensing your Spirit.
> I have no appetite for prayer, Bible study and witness.
> I have lost the plot.

What has happened to the fire which once blazed in my soul?

Where is the peace which passes understanding?
Where is the love that once I knew?
> My heart is cold.
> My soul has shrivelled.
> My mind has become closed up.
> My devotion has died.

Come, Holy Spirit, breathe new life into me.
Let your living waters break out in the depth of my being.
> I want to live and love again!

Amen

4

Broken churches

God himself is diversity in unity. He wants his Church to be one yet also to celebrate its diversity. Look beyond your own local church and seek to engage in mission with partners from other churches and with anyone else who is willing to work with you.

For those who remained, David's departure came as a relief. After two years of tension and argument the end was less dramatic than had been anticipated. David said he was going to pass judgement on the church during the morning service before leading his supporters out. Some lifelong members of the congregation had deliberately stayed away, not wishing to be present at such a painful time. Thankfully it didn't happen like that. David and his group of 20 people failed to turn up. The depleted congregation looked at each other in a state of shock, unsure whether to be sad or glad. The service, conducted by their own minister, proceeded without incident, though members occasionally glanced at the door.

The dispute over 'speaking in tongues' and the 'Toronto Blessing' had torn the church apart. David's house-group had grown in number and vitality following the visit of a friend of his who claimed to exercise a true apostolic ministry. In the months which followed the group had grown increasingly critical of their minister. His 'liberal' views about the Bible had provoked David to interrupt one of his sermons. This triggered the final polarization of the congregation. A split was inevitable after failed mediation attempts. Does the experience of 'new birth' or 'baptism of the Spirit' always have these tragic consequences? Does the new wine always burst old wine-skins?

Family squabbles

In chapter 2 we saw that churches could become shrines and freeze to death. Here we explore the opposite tendency of 'liquid churches' becoming so gaseous that they blow up. The potentiality for splits and divisions was always going to be a problem for John's churches, given their lack of solid structure. A spirit-filled group had broken away from their church. The leaders of this parent church, like scolding fathers, tried to bring their spiritual children back into line. The three letters attributed to John reflect this sad situation. Although written in the third person, 'they' should really be 'you'.

> Children, it is the last hour! As you have heard that antichrist is coming, so now many antichrists have come. From this we know that it is the last hour. They went out from us, but they did not belong to us; for if they had belonged to us, they would have remained with us. But by going out they made it plain that none of them belongs to us. But you have been anointed by the Holy One, and all of you have knowledge. I write to you, not because you do not know the truth, but because you know it, and you know that no lie comes from the truth. Who is the liar but the one who denies that Jesus is the Christ? This is the antichrist, the one who denies the Father and the Son. No one who denies the Son has the Father; everyone who confesses the Son has the Father also. Let what you heard from the

beginning abide in you. If what you heard
from the beginning abides in you, then
you will abide in the Son and in the
Father. (1 John 2.18-24)

Family rows are the worst. We shall see in a later
chapter that the most bitter of these occurred when
Christians were finally banned from the synagogue by
the Jews. Here, things have not reached fever pitch;
Jews and Christians are still talking to each other.
The family squabble is domestic. The letters allow us
to peer through a window and see what is going on in
the family home.

It seems that rival 'liquid churches' were all
claiming to be interpreting the tradition of the
'beloved disciple' through the anointing of the Spirit.
The younger, more fluid, fellowships were flexing
their spiritual muscles. They no longer wished to be
held in check by those old men who had personal
links with the 'beloved disciple'. The breakaway
groups, recalling that the promised Spirit would lead
them into all truth, believed they could approach God
directly without reference to Jesus Christ. Their
spiritual anointing was leading them into a new
freedom; so they left home to do their own thing. The
New Testament regards them as secessionists carried
away on the tide of their own spiritual hubris. The
later Church gave them many brand names like
Gnostisicm, Docetism, Montanism and placed all of
them on the shelf marked 'heretics'. Like an
unpruned vine the Johannine root produced many
runners and an abundance of leaves.

The other mainstream New Testament churches
addressed by Matthew, Luke, Acts and the Pastoral
Epistles were developing a series of apostolic checks
and balances using rules, the authorization of certain
officers and definitions of 'sound teaching'. These
protective walls made them better able to resist

attacks from outside and outbreaks of spiritual anarchy from within. They were building a box for themselves. Drawing on the dynamic tradition of the 'beloved disciple', the writers of John's Gospel chose another route. They wished to introduce future Christians to a more relational model of church in which loving devotion to Christ is central, as once it had been. Jesus is the contemporary animating presence who through his 'other self' as Comforter, personally oversees each member of the flock. Because there was no box, the stability of the community was dependent solely on members being able to bond together in love. Unfortunately there is always a tendency for spiritual children to either copy their parents or cut free from them. The choices our children make sometimes bewilder other family members.

Yet the writers of the Gospel retain high hopes for their church. The world will persecute it but the Comforter (*Paraclete*) will preserve it. Difficulties can be overcome if family members love each other. Sadly our Lord's petition 'that they may be one' was not enough. We catch puzzling glimpses of this within the Gospel text itself. Who, for example, is the group that leaves to dispute over eucharistic matters? Do they break away (6.66) because they cannot share the evangelists' interpretation of the Eucharist? In chapter 10, who are the 'hirelings' who run when trouble comes? They are not the future synagogue leaders of 9.40 who are described as 'thieves and robbers'. Are these 'hirelings' the leaders of other sheep who are not of this particular fold (10.16)? The very mention of 'fold' implies the existence of boxes which the writers think they can transcend.

But there is an additional complication. You may recall from your reading of the Acts of the Apostles (Acts 19.1-7) that Paul had tried to persuade those disciples of John the Baptist who were living in Ephesus to move from water to Spirit baptism. Not all had done so. We have already seen how the Baptist interrupts the flow of the cosmic prologue (1.6-8). He also haunts the opening chapters (1.19-34; 3.22-30; 4.1-3; 5.33-36). Even though he is supposed to decrease his dedicated admirers keep reactivating him.

John's ecumenical dream

The history of the Church is littered with splits, schisms and broken boxes. With depressing predictability what starts off as a 'liquid church' either solidifies or fragments. Organization or evaporation seem to be the only options. The Church on earth will always be like Cinderella, dirty and maligned. This is its nature. Only through faith can we see the Bride of Christ beneath the rags. The painful evolution of John's churches shows us that both 'solid' and 'liquid church' need each other. One provides stability, the other intimacy. The final chapter of the Gospel attempts a reconciliation by introducing the image of an unfragmented net containing fish of all kinds (21.11). The 'beloved disciple' and Peter are shown to exercise complementary ministries. The former has insight while Peter is 'action man'. Peter jumps; the other reflects. Both action and contemplation are necessary.

So what did happen to John's churches? Scholars answer this in different ways. It seems that their theological seeds were somehow planted in the garden of the more solid organized Church. The theological insights were not lost but made their unique spiritual contribution to what was later called the 'Great Church'.

Walls and wells

There are two interesting ways of defining church. You can either start at the edge or at the centre. If you define from the edge you have a reasonable idea of who is in and who is out. Insiders are Christians and outsiders are not. The Church is really a closed box. There is always a welcome since it is not an exclusive club. Nevertheless to be an 'insider' you have to pass some sort of test. You may have to declare something; recite a creed, sign a document, agree a statement or give a testimony. It could be that you have to participate in a ritual like baptism, membership, confirmation or ordination. It may be something about the type of person you are. You are allowed 'in' if you are 'male', or 'straight', white, or someone the 'in-group' knows. The line you cross is subtly drawn, always giving the impression that no formidable barrier exists. Different churches do it in different ways.

John Calvin, one of the Protestant Reformers of the sixteenth century, was not subtle. He simply argued that God had predestined some to salvation and some to damnation. There are hints of this in John's Gospel when Jesus tells his disciples that they have not chosen him but he has chosen them (13.18; 15.16). We also have the exclusive text 'I am the way, and the truth, and the life. No one comes to the Father except through me' (14.6). Although the text may once have been used to draw a line of demarcation between Church and synagogue, it has also led to the construction of all sorts of theological fences. Church leaders, like ecclesiastical policemen, patrol these with great sophistication. The strength of this approach is that both insiders and outsiders know where they stand. An additional advantage is that in times of trouble these fences become walls which protect and preserve those on the inside. Jesus as the Good Shepherd keeps his followers safe within the fold and guards the entrance. Yet he has other sheep who are not in this box. The writers of John's Gospel still retain the dream that walls will disappear so that some day there will be one flock and one shepherd.

These writers also speak of 'wells' and by so doing help us to define church from its centre rather than from its edge. If we picture the Church as a huge bicycle wheel with a hub at its centre and a rim around its edge, then the centre is the 'well' and the rim is the 'wall'. Jesus not only talks to an outsider by a well but likens himself to a 'well-spring' from which people can drink 'living water' (7.37f). When church is defined from its centre we see spokes going out to an uncertain perimeter. You no longer know who is in or who is out because its edges are far away. This type of church is genuinely all embracing. The assumption here is the nearer you are to the 'well-spring' or hub the more Christian you become.

Our Lord's ministry to the Samaritans is presented in this way. A solitary woman comes to the village well, meets with Jesus and a conversation begins. As a result of her testimony the whole village drink living water for themselves and believe Jesus to be the Saviour of the world. Jesus sets no tests for church entry but simply leaves these Samaritans to find their own way. Sadly for John's churches, letting Samaritans in triggered a bitter row in the synagogue between Jewish Christians and their long-standing Jewish friends. This may have been the 'final straw' which precipitated their total exclusion from the synagogue. Even with 'wells' we trip over 'walls'. We are being naive, however, if we think that the 'well' definition of church requires no markers of any kind. Without a rim how do you define the difference between Christians and non-Christians? The Gospel uses the word 'sign'. For John, the fundamental tests are: do Christians 'love one another' (15.12), 'bear much fruit' (15.8) and 'remain with us' (1 John 2.19)? By defining church in this way the number of ecclesiastical engineers required to maintain the walls is reduced. Signs pointing to 'wells' need less servicing than thick 'walls'. The writers are straining to define a church 'beyond the box'.

Ecumenism and ecclesiastical joinery

Professor John Macquarrie, writing in 1975, brought a prophetic critique to the ecumenical vision of his day in *Christian Unity and Christian Diversity.* What he said then is even more relevant today as our culture becomes increasingly liquid. He exposes the ecumenical myth that outsiders are put off by the many different denominations. He says, 'The real evil of division is not diversity but the bitterness and lovelessness to which it can lead, and this can happen within a single church structure as well as between denominations.' In a single denomination, as in a local church, tensions can build until polarization leads to division, as demonstrated in our opening story. This may be happening in the worldwide Anglican Communion as it wrestles with the challenge of 'gay bishops'. Macquarrie argues that we are being superficial if we think a series of ecclesiastical mergers will overcome Christian lovelessness. He goes to the heart of the matter when he says the issue is really about ecclesiastical power:

> One of the most worrying features of the Churches and the ecumenical movement in particular has been the tremendous growth in recent years of ecclesiastical bureaucracy which, one fears, maintains only a very tenuous contact with the actual life of the Church in the parishes.[1]

Like Macquarrie, I no longer believe God is calling us to strive for 'organic union'. This is something given by God alone at the end of history. We do, nevertheless, have to work for 'visible unity' which manifests itself in a common profession of apostolic faith grounded in Scripture and the historic creeds; a complete sharing of baptism and Eucharist; and a common acceptance and interchangeability of ministry and oversight. Attempting to achieve even this vision is proving to be costly in time and energy. It also increases our introspection. Further, it is an irrelevance to a younger generation who are no longer ecumenical but post-denominational. The Church in many parts of the Two-Thirds World is expanding rapidly. This expansion is mainly taking place within the conservative, Pentecostal and evangelical traditions. It is a movement very largely amongst the poor. The western liberal agenda of ecumenism is irrelevant to them as it is to many evangelical churches within our own land. Put at its bluntest; ecumenism is an agenda item for solid, declining 'liberal' church; the young and the growing 'conservative' churches have little interest in it.

Liquid ecumenism

John lays down building blocks for a doctrine of the Trinity. Jesus Christ is described as being at one with the eternal God. It took the 'Great Church' several centuries to develop an acceptable theological formula linking the elements of 'unity' and 'diversity' together within the Godhead. Throughout the twentieth century the western Church struggled to achieve unity. This is hardly surprising given the terrible wars of the superpowers and our growing awareness of being part of a global village. The ecumenical question was 'How can we find a common unity between diverse and divided churches?' In a postmodern liquid culture this question must be restated. 'How can we together as churches celebrate unity and diversity for the common good of the planet and for all people everywhere?' I have suggested in my previous book that God wants to increase diversity rather than reduce it. The dream can in part be realized when we celebrate diversity, rejoice and accept each others' ministry across the denominations, and focus on the world rather than the Church.

We must escape from the small ecumenical box in which we have imprisoned ourselves and return to the original global vision of an ecumenism which embraces the whole inhabited world. Rather than thinking of ecumenism as churches worshipping together we should be looking outwards, focusing upon the Spirit of God at work in the world. We should ask ourselves how we as separate churches can celebrate and co-operate with God in his task of repairing the earth.

A local ecumenical strategy begins when God draws our attention to some felt need within the community. We ask, 'Is God calling us to respond to this need?' Jesus, in his short earthly ministry, did not respond to every situation of human misery. He sometimes refused to act saying, 'My time has not yet come' (7.6; 7.8). There are also references to a particular 'hour' (2.4; 4.21; 4.23; 5.25; 8.20; 12.23). God's time is different from ours. Clock time has seeped into our western souls. Not so in Two-Thirds World countries where village people are more in touch with the rhythms of nature and spirit-life.

Each local church has its own particular time and mission. The trick is recognizing this. As a surfer leaps onto the right wave and is carried along by forces beyond his control, so a particular church has to catch each new wave of the Spirit. Failing to do so not only squanders energy but puts us out of tune with the Spirit. An ecumenical moment happens when God puts the same social concern into the hearts and minds of different people. They are generally the persons we would not choose as partners; indeed, they may not be Christians. In a liquid culture we stay together for as long as it takes. An organization like Christian Aid continues over a long period developing its own organization and structure. The almost spontaneous Jubilee 2000 response to world debt operates more flexibly in waves and unofficial networks. Both of these are modelled on 'wells' rather than on 'walls'.

Ecumenical action

The first step is always to create a space in order to listen to the Spirit. I know of a group of churches who have cancelled all their normal programmes for three months in order to give their active members a chance to recuperate from the relentless demand of turning up for business meetings. Of course, there are dangers. They may so enjoy the space that they will not want to start up again. Outsiders may feel let down and transfer their allegiance elsewhere. Nevertheless, giving a church a 'sabbatical' can have profound implications.

Second, if we sense that we are genuinely being called by God to respond to some particular need, we must recognize that God has already gone ahead of us to prepare others as well as ourselves. This not only confirms that God's universal Spirit is at work but reminds us that he equips those he calls. So we join hands with new partners in planning, discussion and prayer, always remaining open to God. He may wish to take us in new directions. He may invite additional partners to work with us. The time may come when we are called to withdraw, either because this particular work is complete or to allow others to take our place. To work in this way ensures that the whole venture does not solidify too quickly. One illustration will suffice:

In 1996 Keith, the minister, became involved with a family devastated by the impact of their son's drug habit. It became apparent that this was not an isolated case. Household and commercial theft were rampant at the time. Keith's response was to gather together into a 'local action forum' a group of people who were professionally involved with those affected by drug misuse and who therefore had the motivation to do something about it. Among these were a pharmacist, some GPs, the heads of two local secondary schools and other teachers in the primary section. The police attended the bi-monthly meetings, as did representatives of statutory bodies like the Drug Action Team, church leaders, those working with young people and trade representatives. The local MP also supported the work. These people gladly volunteered to give up a couple of hours each month to see what could be done. One thing was certain, this 'forum' was to be no talking shop. If there was no action then the members would quickly disband. Seven years later they are still together. Summing up, Keith asks:

> Have we achieved success? It is difficult to say, and one must be cautious. There are now other programmes in place; policing has changed and so on. However, the number of methadone users locally has fallen, drug-related crime is the lowest for a decade and there is no one using the needle exchange scheme. This would indicate the stabilization of the situation if not an overall improvement. We do not kid ourselves that the war is won. But we have this vision of a community freed

from crime in which young people can grow up without fear that one day someone will be offering them drugs. It is in this context that the Community Drugs Misuse Forum works.

The above is a formal account. When you turn to the next chapter you will read a story of how I was personally caught up in a rather extraordinary way with a very different ecumenical project.

QUESTIONS

1. Have you ever been involved in a situation where Christians have become embroiled in heated disagreements, or have fallen out with each other? What triggered and what maintains the conflict? What constructive steps are possible to bring about a reconciliation?

2. Comment on the suggestion that the real ecumenical question for today is: 'How can we together as churches celebrate unity and diversity for the common good of the planet and for all people everywhere?' What might this mean for your church in terms of its mission?

3. Can you think of any project in which you are involved (not necessarily part of the church's work) which has brought you into contact with colleagues from very different backgrounds? What did you learn from working together?

PRAYERS

Holy Father, whose Son our Lord Jesus Christ
    prayed that his disciples might be one,
forgive us that we have let diversity become
        division,
    and allowed passion to produce polarization.
Forgive us for constructing
    barriers and walls out of bitterness and
        lovelessness.
Look in mercy upon your Church,
    and enable us to work for visible unity
    as, in partnership with others,
    we strive for the common good of the planet
    and people everywhere.

Amen

Holy Spirit,
    within your Church,
        break down the walls which divide us.
        Heal the wounds of our brokenness.
        Renew love in our relationships.
    And lead us from small truths in separation
        to the truth of communion
            in the Father, Son and Holy Spirit.

Amen

5

Martha's keys?

Some of us like to control things while others collude with this. Can we break up existing power bases in order to develop and encourage more creative relationships between different people, giving particular attention to the contribution of the disempowered and those on the margins of society?

I went to the back of the church after pronouncing the benediction. Even though the numbers were small as might be expected on a wet February evening, my message about 'faith' had been well received. The congregation, thanks to a good organist, had sung well. This had been a heavy Sunday but in an hour's time I would be sitting at home by the fire having supper. It was a warming thought. I shook hands and chatted with those who seemed reluctant to venture out into the cold. An Afro-Caribbean lady hovered nearby obviously wanting to speak with me. Having never seen or talked to her before, I approached her.

She came straight out with it. 'Do you believe what you have preached?'

The directness of the question took my breath away. I gave an inward sigh and wondered what lay behind her words.

'Do you believe that if God gives you a vision and you have faith, it will come to pass?'

I fumbled an answer saying something about it depending on the vision and what we understand by faith.

'My name is Constance,' she said. 'You may have heard of me.'

I had.

'God has given me a vision of a women's centre in this town; a safe place where maginalized women who have low self-esteem can "drop in", be accepted, learn to share their skills, gain new ones and recover a belief in themselves. We already have a "drop-in" for men but vulnerable women feel excluded and intimidated when they go there. Besides, I don't want to encourage dependence but rather self-help. You have preached on faith. Do you have enough faith for this?'

Maybe I was thinking of home and supper for I heard myself saying 'Yes.'

'So you do believe?'

I immediately surprised myself by repeating an affirmative 'Yes, I do.'

'Good,' she said, 'because your church has an excellent hall which is under-used during the day and God has told me that he is going to establish the centre there. I would like to start as soon as possible.'

'I have to ask permission of the church council. I think they might consider hiring it out for a trial period.'

'I have no money.'

'Well, they might not require anything until you are well established.' I don't know why I said this because the church nearly always expected payment.

I drove home wondering whether I had been conned. She had a dangerous faith. Had I caught it?

So the 'Women's Centre' was born and five years later won an award from the borough for being one of the most imaginative projects in town.

The women in John's Gospel

> When the wine gave out, the mother of Jesus said to him, 'They have no wine.' And Jesus said to her, 'Woman, what concern is that to you and to me? My hour has not yet come.' His mother said to the servants, 'Do whatever he tells you.' (2.3-5)

> Martha said to Jesus, 'Lord, if you had been here, my brother would not have died. But even now I know that God will give you whatever you ask of him.' Jesus said to her, 'Your brother will rise again.' Martha said to him, 'I know that he will rise again in the resurrection on the last day.' Jesus said to her, 'I am the resurrection and the life. Those who believe in me, even though they die, will live, and everyone who lives and believes in me will never die. Do you believe this?' She said to him, 'Yes, Lord, I believe that you are the Messiah, the Son of God, the one coming into the world.' (11.21-27)

> When Jesus saw his mother and the disciple whom he loved standing beside her, he said to his mother, 'Woman, here is your son.' Then he said to the disciple, 'Here is your mother.' And from that hour the disciple took her into his own home. (19.26-27)

In story after story the women in John's Gospel nudge the men into new ways of seeing. In chapter 2,

Jesus' mother informs him that the wine has run out. However, in Jesus' brutal 'no' she hears a 'yes' and instructs the servants to obey him. In chapters 3 and 4 we have two very different dialogues: one with Nicodemus and the other with a Samaritan woman. Nicodemus, a teacher in Israel, struggles to understand what Jesus is talking about so the conversation quickly fizzles out. The Samaritan woman, on the other hand, has an open, honest theological discussion about living water, the uniqueness of Israel and the mystery of Jesus' person, and pushes the dialogue to a climactic conclusion.

Mary and Martha play a prominent role in the raising up of Lazarus. Some days later, Mary in a generous act of devotion anoints our Lord's feet with costly ointment and wipes them with her hair (12.1-8). Is she the same adulterous woman of chapter 8.1-11, set free from the Law's condemnation through the declaration of Jesus? This anointing is an expression of her love; for Judas it is an incitement to betray. There is a strange resonance between this incident and the account of Jesus' washing the disciples feet (13.2-16). Although the symbols are different the beautiful acts of service are similar. Both actions disturb the men. Are these women modelling true discipleship? They do not abandon Jesus in his darkest hour. His mother, his aunt, another Mary and Mary Magdalene (19.25) watch and wait at the foot of the cross. Where is Peter in all this? He lurks in the shadows. Briefly introduced in chapter 1, Peter appears again in chapter 6, gets it wrong in chapter 13, fights in the garden and then denies Jesus. Whilst the 'beloved disciple' is portrayed as an enigmatic inspirational figure, Peter is presented as a dull cardboard cut-out, lacking insight on every occasion but one (6.69). On Easter Day, although he enters the tomb first, he neither sees nor believes. The first real apostle is Mary Magdalene. It is she who, having seen her risen Lord, is commanded to go and tell the others that Jesus Christ is about to transcend time and space (20.17-18).

Their following of Jesus may not be perfect (Mary Magdalene clings to the risen Christ), nevertheless all these women display key features of discipleship by demonstrating openness, discernment, faith and courageous endurance.

Where are the keys?

Edwina Gateley, in her book, '*A Warm Moist Salty God*', tells a delightful story based on the opening dialogues of John 11. Martha is described as someone who loves shopping, entertaining and trying out her recipes on Jesus and his friends. When Lazarus gets a bug, she writes to Jesus, 'Get over here quick.' But Jesus is busy and leaves it for several days, by which time it is too late. When Jesus arrives finally at the cemetery, Martha, full of repressed anger lays into him. 'Where have you been? You had better sort it out for you are the Son of God.' The result of this interchange is the greatest miracle of all and there in the middle of it is Martha the homemaker who said, 'I believe that you are the Christ, the Son of God' (v. 27). Gateley continues:

> When Peter, the leading disciple, said the same words Jesus responded, 'For this I will give you the keys of the kingdom of heaven.' My question is – where are Martha's keys ... why is it that Peter ended up with the keys and a big statue in Rome when Martha said exactly the same thing and wasn't even noticed! What about Martha? Where's her statue? Does she not also have a claim on the keys of the kingdom? And Peter, after proclaiming his faith in Jesus, denied

that he knew Jesus at all! Three times, no
less. Still, he got the keys and Martha
didn't. Some basic unfairness is going on
here.[1]

The Church from New Testament times has been
controlled by men. This is not to say there have been
no influential women. The formidable St Hilda,
Abbess of Whitby; Hildegard of Bingen, the 'Sibyl of
the Rhine' and Mother Julian of Norwich come to
mind. Often behind a male leader there has been a
significant woman. We have only to think of the
influence of St Clare on St Francis, or Susanna the
mother of John Wesley on her precious son.
Nevertheless, women have usually been confined to
the ecclesiastical kitchen to sing, serve or slave at the
behest of men. Patriarchal pressures have shaped the
nature and culture of the Church so that the
relational has given way to the mechanical and the
intuitive to the rational. Gender issues are, of course,
not as simple as I have made out; nevertheless, I am
sure that if women had been in central leadership
positions within the Church its shape would now be
profoundly different. In John's Gospel, the women
have not yet been pushed to the sidelines. This could
hardly be otherwise in a Gospel pregnant with the
image of 'birthing'.

There is a tradition stemming from Jesus' words
on the cross to his mother and the 'beloved disciple'
(19.26) that when this disciple moved to Ephesus he
took Jesus' mother with him. Even today if you visit
the impressive ruins you can be taken to the site of
'Mary's house'. The writers of the Gospel present her
as a principal witness like the 'beloved disciple',
introducing her into the story following the encounter
with Nathanael (2.1). She not only anticipates the
first sign but is to all intents and purposes instructing
us, the readers, to 'do what he tells you'.

While John's Gospel contains feminine insights it is not a feminist charter. Certainly we can still detect the powerful influence of women behind and in the Gospel but this was soon lost as hierarchical male control put its stamp upon the emerging Church. Thus the relational became organizational; intimacy became papacy; insight became oversight; devotion became promotion in an increasingly centralized bureaucratic institution. Through such means 'liquid church' becomes 'solid church'. These and other excluding forces like those mentioned in the last chapter were at work. We should not put this down to some anti-feminist ideology, rather it reflects a culture in which the testimony of women was given little validity.

A world of connectedness

The prologue of John's Gospel begins by introducing the Greek term 'logos' which is normally translated 'Word'. This is not incorrect yet 'logos' also has a wider meaning. It can refer to 'wisdom'. It has been argued that the prologue has been reshaped from a hymn in praise of wisdom. This wisdom, appearing in holy men and women, is not detached from God but is represented in a person; a female person. God is therefore both male and female and yet transcends gender. Thus at the very start of this Gospel there is a hint of another way of looking at things.

The women in this Gospel remind us of this. John's Gospel contains many polarized opposites: light and darkness, spirit and flesh, truth and lies. The setting of such contrasts in absolute opposition to each other is called 'dualism'. Dualism was prevalent in the Greek thought of the time. This separation of principles has had a profound effect on the way in which western philosophy and science has interpreted the natural physical world. Although technological progress has obviously benefited humankind, there have been some negative consequences both socially and environmentally. We have gained personal independence but have lost our sense of mutual interdependence. The physical earth and even our bodies have become 'objects' rather than sacramental vehicles of spirit and life. We have acquired knowledge without necessarily gaining wisdom.

> The key lies in recovering a sense of connection with all living things, that wide fellow feeling for all that is human. It is my argument that, whenever they have kept alive and vibrant a sense of living contact with natural processes, women have been engaging in the work of redemption on behalf of all humanity. ... Women have discovered a healing strength and wholeness through a range of experiences with nature which offer an alternative to the body/spirit dualism ...[2].

The presence of wisdom and the witness of the women in John's Gospel point to a holistic approach which in overcoming dualism reconnects the physical and the spiritual, the inner and the outer, the rational and the intuitive. The Samaritan woman lures us into a meditation on water and the significance of geographical space and Spirit. Mary caresses the physical body of Jesus as her expensive ointment becomes the sacramental perfume of love. As I have argued elsewhere,[3] everything is relational reflecting the community of Father, Son and Holy Spirit in the Godhead. This means that the salvation of the individual cannot be considered apart from the salvation of the community, neither can the healing of individuals have lasting significance if we are not also environmentally engaged in the healing of the earth.

The wisdom of fools

The feminist theologian Mary Grey, who I have quoted above, drawing on the wisdom tradition, brings a critique to masculine ways of perceiving and knowing.[4] She shows how revelation gets turned into doctrine and then into a set of principles which can be used by the powerful to bully and subdue. Relational and intuitive understandings of truth are obliterated. As a consequence the voices of those who receive wisdom from other sources are silenced. Women so marginalized find it difficult to break out of their imposed silence and even when they do speak they are not listened to. If Pilate had only listened to his wife, Calpurnia, the outcome of the trial of Jesus might have been very different.

Mary Grey quotes the example of the cursed Cassandra of Greek legend. She was a Trojan princess and as a young girl acquired a wisdom which went beyond the patriarchal and militaristic culture of the day. Cassandra alone saw through the propaganda and meaninglessness of the Trojan war even before it began. She warned the people again and again, but they did not listen. So she was forced to live constantly in the angst and the pain. Cassandra, writes Mary Grey, was unable to obtain a hearing because of the Greek dualism, of opposites which allowed no alternative between truth or lies, right or wrong, victory or defeat, friend or enemy. Yet Cassandra, speaking at the centre of the dualism, refused to be a silent victim. In this she speaks for all who have perception but find themselves marginalized.

The testimony of women in John's Gospel cuts through the dualism of light and darkness by proposing a new way of seeing. In doing this the women speak for all on the margins by expressing a relational kind of truth not traditionally acknow-ledged by men. They remind the Church of the necessity of listening to the voices of the mentally ill, the drop-outs, the poor, the homeless, the victims of war and abuse, and those whose sexual orientation is regarded with suspicion by a 'patriarchal church'.

In the gutter

Some scholars looking at chapter 9 see a stitching together of two versions of the story of the man born blind from birth. The first edition reflects a situation where discussions are taking place between Christians and their Jewish friends relating to the identity of Jesus (9.13-17). The second edition, superimposed upon it, comes from a later period when Christians had been ejected from the synagogue (9.34). The Jewish leaders have now made up their minds. Christians are 'the enemy'. Christians reciprocate by giving their opponents a label, calling them 'the Jews'.

This story of healing therefore contains different levels of controversy ranging from critical dialogue to polemical invective. The focus of attention throughout is the blind man and the issue of what has happened to him. For us he represents the marginalized, the poor and the despised of the earth. The women in John's Gospel are at least recognized as persons. This man is treated as an 'object'. He is labelled as someone worthless, fit only for the gutter. His parents further distance themselves from him because they fear the religious leaders. He feels rejected, disabled and dehumanized until he meets with Jesus. Was blindness the fault of his parents or was it his sin? Did something go wrong in the birthing process? Where did the darkness come from? Is it nature or nurture? Even Jesus' disciples treat him as a 'case study' for theological discussion.

Jesus bursts onto the scene as the 'light of the world', turning the value-system of the Pharisees and Jews on its head. He demonstrates that it is the least and the lowest who are the true illuminators of history. This story is a charter for the liberation of the downtrodden and the physically and mentally impaired. Judgement is pronounced on those powerful guardians of closed ideological systems which disable and place people in boxes. What is so remarkable is the way in which this newly empowered man takes control of his own life. He is no longer going to be pushed around or ignored. He is now the subject of his own destiny. He has discovered what it means to live beyond the box. He who lacked sight has insight. When questioned he tells his story without spin or gloss. He refuses to substitute other stories for his own in spite of the taunts, pressure and accusations of others. He can see, they cannot. The story reminds us of Cassandra because, as she experienced, no one believes this man either. The neighbours are intimidated and voice doubts about his identity (9.9). The Jews express their anger and label him as a 'troublemaker'. They will not accept any testimony which challenges what they believe. So they kick him back to the margins from whence he came (9.34).

The story ends in a dialogue with Jesus. The man sees and confesses Jesus to be the 'Son of God'. Like Martha he gets no keys. But more than Martha, he worships. It is the nobodies who shape the history of the kingdom of God. Ultimately they will enable the rest of us to see.

In the church hall

Constance perceived something which neither I nor other members of the church could see. Getting the church council to agree to letting her have the hall for a drop-in centre with only a promise of future payment was not easy. The centre was advertised, opened, the tables set out, the door left ajar. Constance sat and waited. Nothing happened. The weeks went by. No one came. The church council wanted to terminate the arrangement, but help came from one of its members – Deborah. She was a single woman who had a high-powered job with British Airways; a woman of great perception and generosity of heart. I do not know the whole story since Deborah's young life was cut short by cancer. She may have offered to cover expenses, certainly she must have cajoled some members of the property committee. Like Constance she had vision and prayed. Miraculously the trial period was extended. Some of the members, including myself, would drop in to see what was happening. Not much! Few came, maybe two or three a week. On one occasion I challenged Constance as alone she sat waiting. 'Why don't you do something?' She replied, 'I am. I'm praying.' A few months later it really started. In ones and twos women from the street began to trickle in through the doors until the empty hall bubbled with life.

A seed growing

Edwina Gateley, in her book *I Hear a Seed Growing*, describes how, during a time of contemplation in her hermitage in the woods, God called her to go onto the streets of Chicago. There she sought out the homeless who slept in the doorways and the prostitutes who walked the streets, frequented the bars or waited in brothels for customers. The book is full of their painful stories, reflections and conversations. Like the woman at the well, these prostitutes were able to relate to God. Central to the book is Edwina's story of Dolores, a woman in her late twenties who struggled to free herself from the life of pimps, drugs, alcohol, abuse and despairing self-destruction. Edwina gradually comes to the conclusion that only the grace of God can save Dolores. The sadness of her story is that Dolores slips back into the darkness and cannot visualize herself as having a future. She dies in a grubby hotel. Edwina (or is it Dolores) pens a poem offering a woman's picture of God:

God ran away
when we imprisoned her
and put her in a box
named Church.
God would have none
of our labels and
our limitations
and she said,
'I will escape and plant myself
in a simpler, poorer soil
where those who see, will see,
and those who hear, will hear.
I will become a God – believable,
because I am free,
and go where I will.
My goodness will be found
in my freedom and
that freedom I offer to all –
regardless of colour, sex or status,
regardless of power or money.[5]

QUESTIONS

1. Make time and space for an exercise in reflection and imagination. When you feel you have put on one side the pressures and responsibilities of everyday life, focus on three themes only:

   'Someone I know who is outside the normal conventions of my culture, who makes me feel uncomfortable every time I meet them';

   'Someone who evokes my pity because they have been treated cruelly';

   'People I know or people I have heard about who qualify as desperately poor'.

   Share with at least one other person:

   Who you are thinking about under these headings;

   What feelings they provoke in you;

   In particular what you most admire about them, or have learned from them.

2. Are the premises of your church used in any sense like Constance's drop-in centre for the marginalized?

3. When you think about your church, are you satisfied that the distinctive contributions of women (as referred to in this chapter) are allowed to shape the church's life? If not, what has to happen to facilitate their way of doing things and their insights?

PRAYER

We pray for all in our society who are shamed and
marginalized:
the mentally ill and the physically impaired,
the victims of rape and abuse,
the homeless and the drop-outs,
the self-harmers and ex-prisoners,
those who feel condemned because of their
sexual orientation,
those of a different race or culture who feel
discriminated against,
those of another faith who are labelled and no
longer trusted,
those who are driven into prostitution and
crime.
May the compassion of Jesus enfold them.
May the Church be open enough to accept and
embrace them.
May the touch of God release and empower them.
We ask this in the name of God who is the
Father and Mother of us all.

Amen

6

Crazy people

Get stuck into the bigger concerns of social justice. The Church is not meant to be a cosy club but is called to be a prophetic and counter-cultural community.

On the 6 August 2003 a former colleague, the Revd Merfyn Temple, at the age of 84, got on to a plane bound for Harare. He had not told his family what he intended doing because they would have tried to stop him. He had a letter in his pocket which he proposed delivering personally to President Robert Mugabe. The letter reads:

> Dear Mr. Mugabe, The sufferings of the people of Zimbabwe are an abomination in the sight of the Lord. I am praying that the British Government arrest you and charge you with crimes against humanity. Yours faithfully, Merfyn Temple.[1]

It was a crackpot idea, but Merfyn Temple had always been slightly crazy – crazy like Isaiah, Amos, Jeremiah and Jesus. After arriving at the Methodist Church in Harare and reading his letter to the congregation he asked for directions to State House. Leaving all his possessions behind and carrying only a small canvas shopping bag he began his walk. It was a long walk. The streets were empty at that time of day. He met a person and asked the way. 'Keep going,' he was told, 'but you will not be allowed anywhere near. It is protected by the army.' He was stopped, surrounded, questioned and intimidated by the soldiers. The process was repeated several times. Things started to get out of hand. Finally he was bundled into the back of a police pick-up truck and locked up for several days in appalling conditions in Harare's Central Police Station. After further traumas, interrogations and conversations with other incarcerated victims he was released and deported. Only his age and reputation saved him.

There were interesting reactions from church members in Britain when his exploits appeared in the press. Those who had known him for a long time were not surprised; this was the sort of mad thing they expected of him. Some called for a similar prophetic response from Church leaders in this country. Fellow octogenarians saluted him. Official comment suggested that his actions were counter-productive, damaging patient diplomacy and making the lives of ordinary Christians in Zimbabwe more difficult. Those, however, who had been on the inside of Mugabe's jails hoped that the Church might produce more people like Merfyn. The majority of us, I suspect, admired his courage knowing that we would not have the guts to do what he did, but at the same time applied cold logic to his action which some might describe as irresponsible.

Comets and crazy people

Merfyn is one of God's crazy people and 'solid church' has no idea what to do with them. They appear from time to time like comets in the sky. Yet like comets they pass and one wonders whether they have made any difference whatever to the 'real world'. Merfyn's story reminds me of another crazy person who in the late 1950s, when Britain was preparing to explode her hydrogen bomb in the Pacific, decided to protest. Church leaders were also shouting, deploring, passing resolutions and generally pleading with the Prime Minister to desist from such action. A 60-year-old Unitarian, feeling that something should be done, withdrew his life savings, bought a boat and sailed it to the centre of the test area. It was quite idiotic and, of course, it made no difference. But neither did the stamping of official ecclesiastical feet or the noisy protest of churches.

Liberation theology

The Greek word for Church is *'ecclesia'* meaning 'called-out'. Occasionally the Church has to take a stand against some issue of the day and act as a 'counter-cultural community'; a community of protest. It is then that Church leaders 'speak out' and produce carefully worded statements which synod members can support. However, it costs little to put our names to a petition, or stick up our hands after a good debate. We can then congratulate ourselves on being 'prophetic' and move on to the next agenda item. Some of us have been doing this for years, passing resolutions about sanctions, the treatment of Dalits in India, global warming, Two-Thirds World debt, violation of human rights in Burma, the war in Iraq and now Zimbabwe. We want to believe that it makes a difference and sometimes it does. Yet we also need the comets; the signs from beyond; the crazy 60-year-olds who, in personal risk-taking action, galvanize the rest of us into new awareness by turning our words into their costly action.

During the 1960s, some of us read about a new political theology. It was being articulated by those priests and ministers of Latin America who had identified themselves with the poor. They believed that, like Moses of old, God was calling them to speak out against certain economic policies and governmental actions which oppressed human beings. The western Church was suspicious of this 'liberation theology' coming from places far away. Some said its advocates had sold out to Communism. Others, maintaining that religion and politics should not be mixed, argued that religion is a personal matter and that our primary task is evangelism. Those working in the inner cities of this country did recognize its significance.

Today we hear little of liberation theology, though the Jubilee 2000 campaign and the war in Iraq has begun to reawaken our flabby political consciences. Unfortunately, political protests by the Church are given little coverage by the media which often seem more interested in feeding the public obsession with sex-scandals and debates about bishops and homosexuality. Our Christianity is now so privatized that spirituality has become a narcissistic search for self-fulfilment rather than a dynamic engine of social, ecological and political reform. Of course, we continue to pay lip-service to justice issues as befits a counter-cultural community but this remains an insignificant 'optional extra' to normal church activity. These protests, in any case, carry little weight in a culture where words are lost in the cacophony of consumer propaganda. Only the outrageous political actions of crazy persons hit the headlines.

Courtroom dramas

Sections of the earlier part of Nelson Mandela's autobiography, *Long Walk to Freedom*, contain trial scenes, as we might expect of a lawyer. Mandela comments, 'The mills of God grind exceedingly slowly, but even the Lord's machinations cannot compete with those of the South African judicial system.'[2] These courtroom dramas gave Mandela and others banned or imprisoned the opportunity to testify to what the ANC stood for and to confront the state's attempt to label them as dangerous 'terrorists'. Like Jesus in his trial scenes (8.59), the accused managed to escape the clutches of those determined to silence them. The humiliation of the South African Government following the Treason Trial led them to fix the system by appointing their own cronies as judges. They also ceased to observe what they considered to be the legal niceties protecting those on trial. So from 1961 isolations, beatings and torture were adopted to intimidate and elicit information. Using such vicious methods ensured that the defendants could be pronounced guilty.

Jesus represents all victims of political injustice: those imprisoned, tortured and made to disappear through the manipulations of the powerful. In the presence of the Pharisees and the Jews, who represent religious authority, Jesus boldly advances arguments to demolish their theological boxes. His words burn with anger and his indictment of them is radical and terrible. Provoked to a violent rage they try several times to stone him to death (8.59, 10.31). On each occasion he escapes for 'his time had not yet come' (7.30). These fiery dialogues in chapters 5, 7, 8, 9 and 10 are presented as courtroom dramas. The claim that Jesus is 'the Son of God' is debated before us.

Unlike our Roman judicial system the Jewish courts of the first century were not so much concerned to investigate facts as to establish the integrity and competence of the witnesses.[3] The person who produced an impressive array of respected witnesses usually won the case. We see in the other gospels (Matthew 26.60, Mark 14.57-59) that the high priest had a real problem in bringing charges against Jesus at his hastily convened trial because the witnesses did not agree. No charge could have been brought had not Jesus indicted himself.

An informal court was convened by the Pharisees to 'prosecute' (5.16) (not 'persecute' as it is often translated) Jesus for inciting a man to carry his bed on the Sabbath (5.8-10). Jesus defends himself by arguing that his Father has never ceased working and that he Jesus, the Father's Son, is working too. This statement in effect adds blasphemy to the crime of Sabbath breaking. Both offences carried the death penalty by stoning. The writers of John's Gospel wheel in a formidable company of witnesses to persuade us, the jury, that Jesus is indeed 'the Son of God'. The first testimony is provided by John the Baptist (1.34). Next we have the witness of others like Andrew (1.41), Nathaniel (1.49) and Peter (6.69). The women are also witnesses but in a man's world their testimony had no legitimacy. When we enter the trial scenes proper from chapter 5 onwards Jesus brings in his own additional witnesses alongside the Baptist (5.33f). He invokes the testimony of Scripture (5.39), of Moses (5.45) and Abraham (8.33f). He appeals to the signs and deeds he has performed as a living proof that he is from God (10.25). The raising of Lazarus provokes even more dissonance, driving the Jews to 'fix' the system so that Jesus can be silenced for good (11.47f).

While some Pharisees are prepared to concede that Jesus is a teacher sent from God (3.2), the majority will not countenance this since it radically challenges their own understanding of God. The Jews, in their vitriolic antagonism, label Jesus as a 'blasphemer', 'false prophet', 'madman' and 'demon possessed Samaritan' (8.48). Backed into a corner Jesus has no choice but to call upon his chief witness – God, his own Father (8.18, 8.28). By so doing he totally shatters the ecclesiastical mind-set of his judges. They are now condemned by a truth which is beyond them for he has declared himself to be God's cosmic agent, fully representing all that God his Father says and does. A divine voice is also introduced to give validity to Jesus' claim (12.28). The upholders of closed theological systems have only one choice, either to embrace new truth or to destroy the person who operates outside of their theological box.

When Jesus stands before Pilate their conversation is about kingship. Is it of this world or the next? 'Jesus is a dreamer,' concludes Pilate, sacrificing truth to political expediency. He fails to see that if Jesus really is the Son of God then divine kingship will cut right across the rule of Caesar. Jesus in his eyes is no king at all. Brutalized and clothed only in his own vulnerability Jesus is handed over to the baying crowd. From the perspective of John's Gospel, the Church and the world are on trial, not Jesus.

Counter-cultural resources

Merfyn Temple, mentioned at the beginning of this chapter, was incarcerated in a cell designed for six people. There were three filthy bloodstained bunks on either side, two concrete benches and an open stinking toilet hole in the corner. There were 18 men in the cell. A man was dragged in and made to sit on the floor. The guards kept shouting at him and kicking his ankles. Finally they took off his handcuffs, viciously tearing his wrists. He sat whimpering. He had been handcuffed for three days.

The systems of this world do not welcome a radical reordering of their powers. Then as now people are afraid. In oppressive regimes fear paralyses opposition. Jesus lays it on the line that those who stand for the truth will always encounter danger, false witness, threat and persecution (15.18). Yet help is at hand. We will be given a 'new advocate'. The Greek word sometimes badly translated 'Comforter' is 'Paraclete' which literally means someone who has been called to the side of another. The Paraclete is more than a 'helper', 'patron', 'counsellor' or advocate. He is someone whose very presence tells in favour of the plaintiff. As Jesus is God's agent so the Paraclete will be Jesus' agent come to speak up for us when our own words and witness fail. In the farewell discourses of chapters 13-17, Jesus explains how in hostile conditions the advocate will not only replicate his own words but also his deeds (14.12). The disciples now have the same access to the Father as Jesus had (16.26f). It is as if up to chapter 12 the writers of the Gospel are commenting on the negative statement in the prologue, 'He came to his own and his own received him not.' In the farewell discourses they address the positive side, 'to all who received, who believed in his name, he gave power to become ...' (1.12).

Brian Keenan, while visiting Beirut in 1985, was kidnapped by fundamentalist Shi'ite militiamen and incarcerated for four and a half years. In his book, *An Evil Cradling*, he recounts both the horror and the wonder of that terrible period. For some of the time he shared a cell with a fellow hostage, John McCarthy. Without using traditional church language about the Holy Spirit, Brian Keenan appears to be speaking about this Presence:

> At times God had seemed so real and so intimately close. We talked not of a God in the Christian tradition but of some force more primitive, more immediate and more vital, a presence rather than a set of beliefs. Our frankness underlined the reality of our feelings. We were both trying to deal with the force and weight of them. We prayed unashamedly ... In its own way our isolation had expanded the heart, not to reach out to a detached God but to find and become part of whatever 'God' might be. We had each gone through an experience that gave us the foundations of an insight into what a humanized God might be.[4]

The divine advocate promised by Jesus is the principal resource person for threatened disciples. When Christians and persons of goodwill find themselves falsely accused, incarcerated or threatened with death then a supernatural counsel for their defence steps in. This advocate confronts falsehood and as Paraclete tips the balance in the disciples' favour. Ours is a world where many innocent people suffer because of the insatiable greed and lust of the powerful. The writers are pointing to a hidden Presence running through history, upholding justice, passing judgement on evil, embracing the excluded and finally righting the wrongs (16.8-11).

The cuckoo's nest

Ken Kelsy's famous novel, *One Flew Over the Cuckoo's Nest*, describes life in an American mental institution during the sixties. This is a closed world of order, control and categorization. The inmates are given various labels of inadequacy and subjected to the ruthless therapeutic regime of the Big Nurse. Into this grey tyrannical enclosure comes the rough diamond McMurphy, appropriately played in the film version of the novel by Jack Nicholson. He is a brawling, gambling man who wages total war on behalf of his cowed fellow-inmates. One of the acutes, Harding, advises McMurphy not to cause trouble:

> 'This world ... belongs to the strong, my friend! The ritual of our existence is based on the strong getting stronger by devouring the weak. We must face up to this ... We must learn to accept it as a law of the natural world. The rabbits accept their role in the ritual and recognize the world as strong. In defense, the rabbit becomes sly and frightened and elusive

and he digs holes and hides ... He knows
his place.'

[McMurphy replies:] 'Man, you're talkin'
like a fool. You mean to tell me that your
gonna sit back and let some old blue-
haired woman talk you into being a
rabbit?'[5]

The novel reaches its climax when McMurphy
takes 12 inmates beyond the institution on a brief
bout of freedom. The institution then exercises its
final sanction of control by subjecting him to a
lobotomy, chopping away part of his brain and
turning him into a vegetable. In this secular novel
McMurphy, like some Christ-like figure, turns the
cultural assumptions of the institution upside-down
and pays an awful price. Yet the seeds of new life are
sown. Chief Bromden, a half American-Indian whom
the staff believe to be deaf and dumb because he has
remained silent throughout his stay, speaks, smashes
down the door and walks free.

Vanity Fair

Vanity Fair is described in great detail by the
imprisoned John Bunyan.[6] Although it is a city of the
Restoration court this could be a satirical description
of our contemporary consumer society. It is a place
where money rules: a place of getting and spending,
of international commerce, of theme-parks,
amusements, with an underworld of crime and an
overworld of spin. Those living in such a culture
easily become accommodating and compromised.
Pilgrim and his companion are different. 'What will
you buy?' they are asked. They reply, 'We buy the
truth.' They are immediately labelled as crazy people,
incarcerated, judged and condemned.

In our modern 'vanity fair' what or who is the
enemy? Some call it globalization, but how does one

stop this runaway juggernaut which already crashes through every aspect of our culture? Some label it consumerism, but how much fasting and lifestyle adjustments must Christians make before their counter-cultural witness has any effect? This is not to say we should do nothing, yet because the problems are so complex we can become overwhelmed with a sense of futility. A further difficulty arises because the Church itself is so infected with this cultural disease that its prophetic function is paralysed. My examination some years ago of the noticeboard in the foyer of a large middle-class church was revealing. Amongst the profusion of information two forthcoming events caught my eye. One was the church golf tournament, the other a notice from the organizers of Jubilee 2000 inviting church members to join with thousands of others in London for a protest demonstration about reducing Two-Thirds World debt. There were 38 names on the first list and 5 on the second.

From the perspective of militant Islam the enemy is a corrosive mixture of secularism, consumerism, Americanism and Israeli imperialism. In despair a small minority has concluded that you can only attack these monsters by using the terrifying apocalyptic approach of the suicide bomber. Is it possible to fight against the evils within our western consumer culture by methods which are neither futile nor apocalyptic? We breathe the air of this culture; how does one confront an enemy who is both inside and outside of us? One way is to break up this all-enveloping ambiance into its component parts and separately target xenophobia, racism, exclusion, margina-lization, false propaganda, Two-Thirds World debt, and the unjust distribution of wealth. This is a well-trodden path and single issue campaigns do make a difference.

Changing the world

A local Christian Aid organizer called Clive tells of a chance encounter he had in Cologne when members of the G8 were meeting there. Among the thousands of excited protesters who thronged the streets he saw an elderly lady. Her face was covered in war paint. She stood on a low wall banging a drum with all her might. He managed to open a conversation:

'You look as if you're enjoying yourself,' Clive shouted.

'I am! I am! I am! I'm having the time of my life.'

She stopped beating the drum as Clive stood by the wall looking at her.

'I'm Clive,' he said.

'I'm Ida,' she replied. 'And I'm 84.'

'Hello, Ida. Where do you come from?'

'I'm from Tunbridge Wells in England.'

Clive was a little taken aback. She did not conform to his image of senior ladies from Tunbridge Wells.

'I've attended the church all my life,' said Ida. 'I have organized coffee mornings, sung in the choir, washed up in the kitchen, and worked hard for the Christmas Fayre. When I reached 80 years old I asked myself, what have I done with my life? I sadly concluded, not much. It was after this that the Jubilee 2000 campaign caught my imagination. I'm blessed with good health and decided that I should do something while I still had the strength.'

'So what are you doing?' asked Clive.

She immediately began beating the drum and yelling at the top of her voice, 'I'm changing the world! I'm changing the world, I'm changing the world!'

At the margins

Jesus established solidarity with the powerless. While most of us have become so compromised that we cannot focus, those driven to the margins do have some idea of the systems and people who have driven them there. Their labelling of the evils within our society may be inaccurate but they stand a better chance than we do of naming what has put them there. The Church will become a counter-cultural community only when it gets alongside the poor and the excluded. To do this Christians must leave their comfort zone and go beyond the box. The Church will find renewal when it incarnates itself at the margins where the stranger, the deprived and the powerless dwell. The excluded are not only found in our inner cities but are scattered across rural areas and hidden in the rich suburbs.

Jeremy was puzzled that Age Concern delivered meals to this impressive house. The family living there was obviously well-to-do. There were two BMWs in the drive and it looked as if a new extension had recently been added to this three-quarters of a million pound property. Jeremy had been told to take the meal around the back. He crunched across the gravel, through the garden gate which had been left unlocked, found the door and knocked. He called and entered. He was immediately in a dingy room. Here sat Anna, a frail yet rather grand lady in her eighties. This large house had once been hers but her son and daughter-in-law had taken it over. Bit by bit they had pushed her into this dismal room which had become a sort of granny flat. They never called to see her or bothered to ask how she was. Even the two teenage grandchildren who still lived in the house no longer visited her. Her only lifeline was the telephone, the occasional visit of the nurse and Age Concern. Jeremy delivered the meal and came away feeling very angry.

For Jeremy, anger was a wake-up call. The niceness of his suburban surroundings had papered over the pain and hidden the social exclusion. He had not experienced anger like this for some time and it made him feel uncomfortable. He had been told that Christians should not get angry. These stirring emotions were threatening to shatter his cosy do-gooding box. He remembered that Jesus got angry too. His own anger did not seem like righteous anger, but it did make him want to do something. Benevolent charity was not enough. How many other lonely and excluded people lived in his neighbourhood? He realized that he had a new agenda.

QUESTIONS

1. Who are the groups in your neighbourhood who come to mind when you hear about 'the stranger, the poor, the deprived and the voiceless'? What can Christians do locally to identify with them?

2. What action will you take, however small, which might make a difference to the large issues of injustice and oppression in today's world?

3. In a world of competing interpretations of the causes and the cures of contemporary ills, how is the 'prophetic voice inspired by God's Spirit' to be discerned?

PRAYERS

I have become too comfortable.
> I have privatized my faith and emptied it of sharp prophetic content.
> I am content with my cosy church and sanitized gospel.
> I have lost touch with the poor, the stranger, the lost and the despised.
> My lifestyle is little different from non-Christians who are similarly trapped in a culture of want and desire.

Help me to ask radical questions about the world in which I live.

Help me and others in my church to see what can be done to make a difference.

Help me to have the courage to make an intelligent and appropriate stand for justice and righteousness.
> Through Jesus Christ, the liberator of all who are oppressed.

> > Amen

Lord of justice and freedom,
> We pray for all prisoners of conscience
> > and for all those wrongly incarcerated or cruelly tortured.
> We pray for judges and those who seek to promulgate and maintain
> > just laws and the protection of human rights
> > > in the face of oppressive governmental regimes.

We pray for Christians who are persecuted for
    their faith
      and for those religious minorities who feel
      victimized and fearful.
May justice and truth prevail as the streams of
    God's righteousness
reorder the powers of this world
    bequeathing to each person and community
    peace and hope.

                                      Amen

7

Passion and petition

Discipleship may demand costly sacrifices. Pray and obey. There is no other way of expressing our love and commitment to Jesus.

It was a breathtaking moment. The silence in the Royal Festival Hall was palpable as we waited for the Bach Choir to sing 'Be near me, Lord, when dying'. I first heard a performance of the St Matthew Passion in this building 40 years before. The pattern of performing part one in the morning and part two in the afternoon has remained unchanged. The interpretation of this Bach masterpiece has shifted over the years, becoming more delicate as the orchestral forces have been scaled down. The silence following the evangelist's announcement that Jesus 'yielded up the ghost' remains as pregnant as ever.

Two days before, I had sat in a cinema watching Mel Gibson's *The Passion of the Christ* where a brief pause was attached to the moment of Christ's agonizing death. This silence was quickly followed by the Hollywood theatricals of a falling tear, an earthquake and the scattering of Christ's foes with a hint of resurrection. These flashes of hope hardly ameliorated the relentless and unremitting punishment inflicted on Jesus and vicariously on the cinema audience. Such an enigmatic victory failed to obliterate the abiding image of the lacerated body. While devotional love and the luminosity of joy pervades Bach's epic, shock and horror crown Gibson's presentation.

Both of these presentations of the passion are creative. They belong together. Just as each of the gospels add their own slant to the Jesus story reflecting the situations out of which they were written so these two presentations tell us something about context. The first is a product of an eighteenth-century chorale-singing Protestantism. The second is a commentary on our violent twentieth century. Bach's performance has cleaned up the blood and guts. Mel Gibson has glorified torture so that Christians can no longer hide from its horror in some cosy religious box.

Passion contexts

> Meanwhile, standing near the cross of Jesus were his mother, and his mother's sister, Mary the wife of Clopas, and Mary Magdalene. When Jesus saw his mother and the disciple whom he loved standing beside her, he said to his mother, 'Woman, here is your son.' Then he said to the disciple, 'Here is your mother.' And from that hour the disciple took her into his own home. After this, when Jesus knew that all was now finished, he said (in order to fulfil the scripture), 'I am thirsty.' A jar full of sour wine was standing there. So they put a sponge full of the wine on a branch of hyssop and held it to his mouth. When Jesus had received the wine, he said, 'It is finished.' Then he bowed his head and gave up his spirit. (19.25-30)

In John's Gospel, Jesus endures suffering in such a regal way that it appears not to affect him. The terror has been tamed and the suffering sanitized. His passion performance is a march of triumph evoking admiration and wonder. Of course, some brutalization remains. Before the high priest, Jesus is struck on the face; but only once. The writers, following Mark and Matthew, record the scourging, the crown of thorns and mockery of the soldiers (19.1). There is, surprisingly, no cry of dereliction from the cross and no noisy taunts from the crowd or the priests. The latter only lodge a complaint to Pilate about the inscription 'King of the Jews'. While scenes of frenzied activity cluster around the crucifixion in the other gospels, John's cross is bathed in contemplation and climaxes with the triumphant shout 'It is finished.' Nevertheless the writers add glosses of their own. The beloved disciple, rather than Peter or the brothers of Jesus, is appointed son and heir of the Jesus tradition along with Mary. These final events are also shown to fulfil the Scriptures which act as a witness to his glory. The garments are divided, the wine-vinegar is drunk, the leg bones are not snapped and our Lord's side is pierced; all in accordance with the Scriptures. There is also the witness of the blood, the water and the breathing out of the Spirit. These signs are meant to offer crucial evidence against the dualistic idea that Jesus Christ only had the appearance of fleshy humanity (1 John 5.7f).

A dangerous world

Mention of the seamless robe is an important sign. Commentators differ over its significance. Some regard it as a priestly vestment and by linking it with the hyssop plant suggest that the writers are flagging up the priestly work of Christ. Alternatively, could this bloodied undergarment represent the seamless robe of the Church which was to find its way into the Roman world? The Church, as we saw in chapter 4, was anything but seamless. Christ's crucified body was scarred and bloodied but not broken. It too may symbolize hope for a united Church.

When Jewish Christians brought Samaritan Christians into their synagogues there was such an explosive conflict that both were kicked out. I suspect that this may have been the incident which triggered the re-editing of the Gospel and the inclusion of material which ratcheted up the antagonism between Christian and Jew. Jesus himself is now accused of being a Samaritan (8.48). Bitterness between Judaism and Christianity continued in mutual recrimination. 'They will put you out of the synagogues. Indeed, an hour is coming when those who kill you will think that by doing so they are offering worship to God' (16.2). Judaism had been tolerated in the Roman Empire. As long as Christians remained Jews, the Roman authorities had not bothered them. However, when followers of Christ were no longer regarded as Jews their failure to adhere to pagan customs got them into trouble with the State. All this hostility from outside produced a fortress mentality within. It seemed that the world hated them (15.18) because they no longer belonged to it. 'If they persecute me,' said Jesus, 'they will persecute you also' (15.20). 'But,' says John, 'don't get depressed, Jesus has overcome the world' (14.30, 16.33). It didn't feel like that.

Since 9/11 uncertainty, insecurity and fear has infiltrated the complacent cultures of the US, Britain and Europe. Our world has become an even more dangerous place since the invasion of Iraq. Apocalyptic fantasies, some spawned by the book of Revelation, fuel fortress mentalities in communities, countries and churches. Attempts to destroy the dandelions of terror have scattered their potent seeds across the western nations. Instead of one identifiable Saddam monster we now have thousands. The threat of a sudden terrorist attack haunts western populations. The dualism of light and darkness, references to the prince of this world and hostility to outsiders, all of which are found in this Gospel, have a contemporary ring. Even the horrors described in the book of Revelation can be made to fit the machinations of nations and the mechanisms of modern warfare. Fragmentation, isolation and bloodied flesh stain our contemporary existence.

God's tears

Trevor Dennis, in his book *Imagining God*, tells a beautiful story about Noah's animals.[1] They are lined up leaning over the rails of the ark staring into the watery deep. They no longer move or say anything. At the beginning of their great adventure they had frolicked and played. In their early excitement they had even forgotten old enmities. As the primal waters swallowed up the earth a great sadness fell upon them. The kangaroos no longer jumped, the nightingales stopped singing, and the dolphins lay drifting on a timeless sea. Noah and the other humans, overcome with shame, had locked themselves in their cabins. One morning one of the antelopes, staring at the perpetual rain, said, 'We are adrift on an ocean of God's tears.'

In my book, *Into the Far Country*, I reflect on the rainbow covenant which God made with Noah after the holocaust of the flood.[2] Ancient mythological stories recount this primal event. Whatever the facts, this story has become revelatory. God, who is initially portrayed as losing his patience, releases the watery chaos because he is fed up with human corruption and violence. Only Noah, his family and a travelling zoo are preserved. Yet love wins through as God regrets his hasty action. He will not do it again. The world's pain and his own accountability for contributing to it will remain indelibly printed on his heart. Yet at the end of December 2004 a tsunami of violent waters again reeked destruction upon millions, casting their dead upon the seashore. It was as if God had forgotten his rainbow promise. This I cannot believe! What has happened is not his pronouncement of judgement upon us. Divine judgement has already fallen upon Jesus Christ. The tsunami was, rather, a salutary reminder that we live a precarious existence on an unstable planet where forces of order and chaos mingle. We who live in cosy boxes tend to forget this. The Indian Ocean disaster can be viewed as a reminder and a wake-up call. Jesus Christ shows us that we are only truly human when the pain of others touches us.

The Bible message is about a passionate God who, entering the pain and mess, chooses to dwell in the violent vortexes of our earthly existence. This God takes into himself the brokenness of the Church, the fragmentation of humanity and the agonizing loss of the tsunami victims. Such a God is capable of pain, joy and suffering; a 'Living God', not the amoral metaphysical creation of the Greek philosophers. This is not the managing-director God who lives beyond the sky but the God who is lost in the storm. Because the 'Word' (*logos*) has replicated itself in bleeding flesh, the capacity for pain and tears is shown to have been in the heart of God from the beginning. He is present 'to us' as eternal joy, but he is also present 'with us' in vulnerability, particularly so amongst the marginalized, the bereaved, the lost, the widows, the orphans and the victims of flood and oppression. In him, hurt and hope so coalesce as to bring about the redemption of all things. The pathos of God in the Old Testament is but the presupposition for the passion of God in the New. God weeps when bloodied flesh is torn from his Son's back, as Mel Gibson so graphically portrays in his film. The tears of God for a bleeding world continue to splash upon our poisoned earth.

Geoffrey Studdert Kennedy was an army padre in the First World War. He was better known as 'Woodbine Willie' because he handed out cigarettes to the troops in the soaking mud-filled trenches of Flanders. He puts what I am trying to say into a rough rhyme:

> I wonder if God sheds tears,
> I wonder if God can be sorrowin' still,
>> And 'as been all these years.
> I wonder if that's what it really means,
>> Not only that 'E once died,
> Not only that 'E came once to the earth
>> And wept and were crucified?
> Not just that 'E suffered once for all
>> To save us from our sins,
> And then went up to 'Is throne on 'igh
>> To wait till 'Is 'eaven begins,
> But what if 'E came to the earth to show,
>> By the paths o' pain that 'E trod,
> The blistering flame of eternal shame
>> That burns in the heart o' God?
> O God, if that's 'ow it really is,
>> Why, bless ye, I understands,
> And I feels for you wi' your thorn-crowned 'ead
>> And your ever pierced 'ands.[3]

The tears of Jesus

'Jesus wept' (11.35). There are only two occasions when Jesus weeps, though Mark in his Gospel portrays Jesus experiencing turbulent emotions of anger, pity and terror. Luke describes Jesus weeping over Jerusalem (Luke 19.41) as he foresees the approaching doom. He longs to embrace his people, but they will not come (Matthew 23.37). Jesus weeps at the tomb of Lazarus. Are these the tears of sympathy? Does he weep because of his poignant love for them? This makes no sense. The tragic situation, as Martha so rightly points out in her scolding rebuke, could have been avoided if Jesus had not taken so long in getting there. Is he therefore crying his own tears of remorse because he is responsible? Clearly he is very troubled in spirit. The Greek words suggest deep agitation. There is certainly anger at the unbelief of the Jews, sorrow that death's shadow has fallen on those he loves, fear that the escalating violence is about to sweep him and his disciples into an abyss. This prompts the fundamental question: why did he allow Lazarus to die? John's answer is clear; it is so that Jesus himself will be glorified. 'Glorification' is the writers' word for death and resurrection. Put another way, glorification reveals the timeless crucifixion at the heart of God. The resuscitation of Lazarus will cost Jesus his life (11.45-50). There will be no more Houdini acts of disappearance and escape as in previous confront-ations with the Jews. This action guarantees his death. Death will not be sleep but a terrible journey into a primal void and out the other side, so that resuscitation is transcended by resurrection. The grave clothes will be left behind as a reborn Christ leaps forth into boundless freedom beyond the box. Jesus weeps because God sheds tears. The cross existed in the heart of God long before it was planted on Golgotha's hill.

George Matheson (1842-1906), best remembered for his evocative hymn 'O love that wilt not let me go',[4] was a parish minister whose blindness drove him at times to near despair. His experience of loneliness and suffering forced him with inner eyes of faith to meditate upon the sufferings of Christ and the sacrificial power of the cross. In his blindness he came to see that Christ slain from the foundation of the world was the central animating principle of the universe. From water and blood comes ecological life. It turns seeds into flowers, darkness into light. In the storm clouds, wind and tempest, rainbow glories of grace are displayed. There is an evolutionary process at work in the ecological mechanisms of the world fed by sacrifice and tears producing a 'fall upwards'. Unlike the pessimistic message of Thomas Hardy, Matheson believed the universe to be impregnated with hope. All humanity will at length be freed from abnegation and self-love.

Pain and petition

In the earlier part of John's Gospel there is no reference to Jesus praying. As the sharp exchange between Jesus and the Jews intensifies we begin to sense another, more intimate dialogue going on between Father and Son. Finally Jesus openly weeps and prays for the benefit of the people (11.42). This inner dialogue reaches its glorious climax in the farewell discourses. Here Jesus gives us powerful incentives for intercession:

> I will do whatever you ask in my name, so that the Father may be glorified in the Son. If in my name you ask me for anything, I will do it (14.13f).

> If you abide in me and my words abide in you, ask for whatever you wish, and it will be done for you (15.7).

> On that day you will ask in my name. I do not say to you that I will ask the Father on your behalf; for the Father himself loves you, because you have loved me and have believed that I came from God (16.26-27).

The phrase 'in my name' is central to these petitions. What does it mean? Is it simply an efficacious postscript attached to the petition to guarantee results? The divine name I AM, revealed first to Moses and then taken up by Jesus, expresses the character, nature and being of God. The person is in the name. Intercession in the name of Jesus means that we identify ourselves with him just as he has identified himself with the Father. We stand where he stands in the same place of pain. Effective petition springs from a deep intimacy with Jesus and a solidarity with marginalized victims. In the high-priestly prayer of chapter 17 Jesus repeatedly uses the word 'know' to describe the relationship between himself and the Father. In the Old Testament this word is often used to describe sexual intercourse. In John 'know' is used to portray the interdependence and the interpenetration of Spirit, will, mind and being in the relationship between Father and Son. When we pray 'in his name' we are no longer external observers but partners drawn so intimately into the pain and purpose of the trinitarian God that our minds and wills are reconformed to his. Prayer means doing what Jesus did. Petitions are purified by obedience.

> By telling his disciples that they, too, will
> be persecuted,
> Jesus is revealing how they are called to
> become like him.
> They too will accomplish the works of
> God.
> Not just through powerful words and
> wisdom
> but through their weakness, failure and
> even death.
> They will give life as Jesus gave life.
> They will conquer the world not in a
> visible way,
> but through their littleness and poverty ...
> So, too, all those who are called to give
> their lives for Jesus,
> for truth and for justice, become like him.

They, too, live that hour of Jesus.
Their shed blood becomes one with the
    blood of the crucified Jesus.
Their blood waters the arid land of our
    hearts
to bring forth new life.[5]

A young Christian recounted how she prays for a parking space which God always provides. I believe God wants us to grow up as mature partners and leave such childish dependence behind. God wants to enlarge and deepen our petitions. He does this by demanding costly obedience. Prayer becomes harder as the Spirit seeks to draw us into the truth. In the high-priestly petition of Jesus he prays that we be 'sanctified by the truth' (17.17). 'What is truth?' asks Pilate. The answer stares him in the face, for truth and death are intimately related. The truth of Jesus belongs to a world where his servants do not fight but weep (18.36). His mission establishes a kingdom which is neither undermined nor achieved by violent means. To pray 'in his name' is to be part of the world's pain. Once there we will no longer be bothered about parking spaces or the health of our pet rabbit but instead be identified with the traumatized, the victims of war, AIDS, tsunami, and those who work at the borders of life and death. We will be praying for the breaking of the powers of evil at work in powerful men like Pilate who turn the marginalized into victims. Western Christianity suffers more from smallness than from sin. Missionary petition 'in his name' replaces triviality with depth, cosiness with frustration, complacency with mortality, easy answers with mystery, security with death. Such petition, while pointing us to the void, also places us at the heart of the Trinity.

There are two simple instructions for those who engage in mission: 'pray' and 'obey'. Of all the obligations this is the simplest and the hardest.

A theological story

Howard was in hospital again. Over the past six months it seemed as if his whole existence had revolved around hospital appointments. Would tomorrow's operation be successful? He sat by his bed surveying others in the ward. He knew a little about each from the snatches of conversation he had overheard. As so often happens in hospital, he realized that others had conditions more serious than his own. Life from a hospital bed is a levelling experience. Here, people from different backgrounds are gathered together to wait, hope and learn the truth about themselves, bound by a common experience which has disrupted normality and stained them with mortality. Here is 'alternative church'; maybe more church than the 'normal church' he attended on Sundays. Such thinking was not something he could easily share with his congregation for Howard was a minister. He was expected to be the confident carer. It was assumed that fear, doubt and vulnerability did not touch him. To tell the truth, he was afraid. He disguised this by his cheerful manner. How much longer did he have to live? He so much wanted to see Derek and Jean, his children. He had not spent as much time with them as he ought to have done. Ministry seemed to have got in the way. Would they now have time for him? Above all he missed Sylvia, his wife.

Into the ward strode his boss, the Superintendent Minister, like a general surveying his troops. He radiated goodwill and confidence, dispelling anxiety and gloom. Howard got on well with him and respected him. It was strange watching him do what he so often had done on his ministerial hospital visits.

This minister's friendly manner brought warmth to the ward. He did not ignore the other patients as he made his way to Howard. He spoke to a few of them again when he left. Howard appreciated this visit, even the prayer which can create embarrassment in an open hospital ward. Yet when he had gone, Howard felt a tingle of anger intensifying within him. What had prompted this? He had told Howard of a group who were holding a prayer vigil for him and that he would be surrounded by prayer next day when he went in for his operation. Did this trigger these negative feelings? It was good to feel at the centre of prayer; to be a receiver of grace rather than a giver. Prayer did make a difference. He knew from past experience. Why, then, did he feel uneasy and angry? Then in a flash he saw it. It sprang from what he, his Superintendent and people in church believe about intercessory prayer. He did not doubt its power, so why should it be focused on him and not on others? There was unfairness here. Intercessory prayer had become parochial when it should be universal.

In mission we are called to work with God in bringing wholeness to all humanity. We are called to live inside the high-priestly prayer of John 17 where universal 'knowing' and 'loving' dwell in the relationship between Father and Son. All prayer has to be inclusive and universal *before* it can be localized and particular. That is why the Lord's Prayer begins 'Our Father' and why 'our and us' reoccur in all the petitions. Howard saw this. But there was a further puzzle. Was it fair of God to answer prayers for him and to ignore the needs of others simply because they were not the focus of prayer? Why does God heal some who pray and yet seems to do nothing for the majority of humankind who suffer and die of starvation and malnutrition each day? Is God so busy elsewhere, as Jesus was in the Lazarus incident, that he allows some people to die? Does God not act for others because he cannot, or because he will not?

The next morning Howard was wheeled into the operating theatre. He was third on the list. He had chatted to the other patients in the ward, attempting to allay their anxieties. They appreciated his presence. He gave a final cheery wave as he left the ward for the last time. I say the last time for Howard did not return. He died on the operating table.

Jesus wept.

QUESTIONS

1. Some typical human reactions when a loved one becomes seriously ill: 'Keep your spirits up, it will help you pull through'; 'The doctors are doing all they can'; 'I cannot face this, my whole life is in tatters'; 'I know what's to blame for this mess'. Where in the midst of these feelings, and others like them, is the focus of Christian prayer?

2. How do we discern what God wants of us in regard to situations of grief and suffering?

3. What do we really think is going on when we pray?

PRAYER

Don't hide,
don't run,
but rather
discover in the midst of fragmentation
a new way forward:
a different kind of journey
marked by fragility,
uncertainty
and lack of definition.
And on that path
to hold these hands
that even in brokenness
create a new tomorrow.[6]

Lord God,
I find it hard to believe when an earthquake shakes the ocean and towering waves destroy the homes of thousands, scattering their dead upon the seashore.
I cannot say, 'Thy will be done' when the untamed violence of nature erupts and devastates the earth, denying your pronouncement of good upon creation.
I can only believe if you are in the mess and share the traumas of earth's peoples.
I can only have faith if you take the blame and suffer the pain of your troubled world.
BUT THIS YOU HAVE DONE!
So I know a cross existed in the heart of God, before it was planted on Calvary's hill.
So I recognize grief in eternal love, how repentant scars wound the holy will.
As you weep, I worship you; and our sorrows, mingling with the tears of millions, draw hope in humanity and healing to the earth.

Amen

8

The beckoning silence

Let's move out of the comfort zone. We and our churches must wrestle with deeper issues and begin to talk to outsiders about God, so that they too can become disciples of Christ.

It is two o'clock in the morning. I am staying with my son in one of the London University student halls of residence. Some students have decided to hold a party in the corridor. As the noise level rises my irritation increases. Yesterday was bad. It was hard saying goodbye to my wife Christine, knowing that I would not be seeing her for several months. On the coach from Manchester I had realized that if my time journeying across India and Sri Lanka was not to become a nightmare I would have to let go of my desire to control and learn how to react positively to the unexpected.

I was burdened with a catalogue of scare stories. People who had been to India recounted these with relish. I heard of luggage stolen, touts and con men taking you where you did not wish to go, the dangers of being robbed, the real possibility of illness and fever. The list was endless. I was repeatedly told: 'You must make sure that the water you drink is boiled.' My heavy case is full of clothes, medicines and articles for every eventuality. Around it is a large chain and padlock to discourage thieves. As I contemplate my tightly bound possessions I realize that I too am locked up. I am fearful. I regret my decision to embark on such an adventure with no guide, no language and with an uncertain itinerary. Surely I should have chosen the safer option and gone on a package holiday? To make matters worse the latest bomb blast in Colombo – where I hope to stay initially – has meant that it would be unsafe for Christine to join me there. My stress levels are high.

Martin laughed when he lifted my case. 'It weighs a ton. Surely, Dad, you don't intend to lug this all over Asia?' So for the third time I unlock it, remove further articles and finally decide to abandon the chain. I have to let go. I must risk it. I must learn to trust. Isn't this what the journey is all about?

Journeys beyond the box

> Simon Peter said to him, 'Lord, where are you going?' Jesus answered, 'Where I am going, you cannot follow me now; but you will follow afterwards.' Peter said to him, 'Lord, why can I not follow you now? I will lay down my life for you.' Jesus answered, 'Will you lay down your life for me? Very truly, I tell you, before the cock crows, you will have denied me three times.' (13.36-38)

What luggage do you take when you embark on a spiritual and theological journey? It depends on the type of journey; for you have two options. The first is the pilgrimage, fraught with risks and uncertainties as you travel beyond the box. The second, the package tour, guarantees new experience with maximum safety within the box. The journey is clearly mapped out from the start, transport is organized and you are promised clean accommodation. If there are difficulties your attentive guide will sort it out. There are some beautifully reassuring promises of spiritual package in John's Gospel.

> 'Do not let your hearts be troubled. Believe in God, believe also in me. In my Father's house there are many dwelling-places. If it were not so, would I have told you that I go to prepare a place for you?

> And if I go and prepare a place for you, I will come again and will take you to myself, so that where I am, there you may be also. And you know the way to the place where I am going.' Thomas said to him, 'Lord, we do not know where you are going. How can we know the way?' Jesus said to him, 'I am the way, and the truth, and the life. No one comes to the Father except through me. If you know me, you will know my Father also. From now on you do know him and have seen him.' Philip said to him, 'Lord, show us the Father, and we will be satisfied.' (14.1-8)

> 'I have said these things to you while I am still with you. But the Advocate, the Holy Spirit, whom the Father will send in my name, will teach you everything, and remind you of all that I have said to you. (14.25-26)

The tourist guide (Paraclete) will be there with you. Hotels and 'dwelling places' are all booked in advance to reduce anxiety. The country you are visiting may have its dangers but Jesus has gone ahead to prepare the way since he is 'the way, and the truth, and the life'. This statement has been used to encapsulate the Christian package of salvation. Its distinct emphasis guarantees an exclusive life-giving experience and ensures that no other tour operators muscle in on your journey to God's wonderland.

However, what may appear to be a package is qualified by small print which turns it into something else. Theological packages always turn out to be self-limiting. That is why Jesus invites us to break out and live 'beyond the box'. Philip, Thomas and Peter are scared and bewildered by this. The statement 'I am the way, and the truth, and the life' is not about a package after all, but is a ticket for a mystery tour where the destination is unknown and the risks impossible to assess in advance. We therefore have no idea how to prepare and may well discover that the theological luggage we take with us is either too heavy or totally unsuitable for the terrain we are exploring.

No theological package could have prepared Howard for his final day in hospital. His unexpected death deconstructed the theological frameworks of the Superintendent and Howard's church members. In the ward Howard had been improvising, using fragments of previous theological systems as the raw material for reflecting on his current situation. It was preparing him for the total abandonment of systems of every kind, beckoning him to undertake the final journey beyond the box.

When the risen Lord came to his disciples he instructed them to move. 'As the Father has sent me, I send you' (20.21). Born again Christians are driven by the Spirit from their natural home. Their sending replicates the sending of the Son by the Father. They leave a familiar world to enter an unfamiliar one. The word 'mission' comes from the Latin '*mittere*' meaning 'to send'. It describes movement from one place to another. John's Gospel is saturated with 'sending' words. God sends Jesus and Jesus sends his disciples (3.17; 5.36-37; 6.44, 57; 8.16, 18, 26; 10,36; 14.24; 17.18; 20.21). Mission for us today is seeing where God is at work and joining in.

This Gospel, because of the manner in which it has been assembled, has Jesus journeying backwards and forwards between two contexts, the countryside of Northern Galilee and the urban world of Jerusalem. He starts at Bethany (1.28), moves across to Galilee

(1.43) calling in at Cana (2.1) before visiting Jerusalem (2.13). He returns to the Judaean countryside (3.22) and travels through Samaria (4.4) before coming back to Cana (4.43). We next find him in Jerusalem (5.1) then on the other side of the Sea of Galilee (6.1) before he walks across the water to the synagogue in Capernaum (6.59). This criss-crossing continues right up to the concluding climax in Jerusalem. These movements have theological rather than topological significance. They are missionary journeys across several cultural settings. Jesus is not only a man from another world, the home of the Father, he is a man exploring the different cultural contexts of this world. He is similarly calling us to live beyond our own cultural box. In mission such horizontal movement opens us up to the possibility of discovering God in the most unexpected places. This, however, is not the most significant movement for the writers, they are more interested in the vertical motion of 'downreach'.

Downreach

There is 'downreach' in the sense of 'reaching down' as a servant. Jesus, knowing that the Father had put all things under his authority, exercises power by abandoning it and by kneeling before his disciples 'showed them the full extent of his love' (13.1). As we have seen, the men in John's Gospel are not good at this. Peter objects when Jesus, abandoning his outer garments, stoops to wash his feet, thereby giving him a personal example of how disciples should behave. Even when he sees the risen Lord on the seashore (21.7) Peter wraps his outer garments around him to cover his vulnerability before leaping into the water. Jesus challenges him repeatedly. 'Do you love me?' 'Downreach' involves casting off power as we understand it and embracing our own and other people's vulnerability.

Evangelism is sometimes called 'outreach'. The implication is that disciples move out from their own familiar church culture in order to pull outsiders back into it. This activity is often an 'add-on' to normal church. It is hardly surprising that busy church members are not keen. Attending Sunday worship, fitting in the housegroup, going to business meetings, attending coffee mornings, holding office or doing a church job can swallow massive amounts of time. How does one fit 'outreach' into such a crowded diary? This Gospel portrays evangelism as 'downreach'.

We saw in chapter 5 how the Word (*logos*) comes as wisdom and light, enabling a new way of seeing. This same *logos* also comes as 'word', enabling conversation beyond the box. *Logos* lies at the heart of every meeting between people and is present in all the interactions and encounters we have with one another as well as with animals, plants, trees and created things. *Logos* can therefore be discovered inside of every 'dialogue'.

'Downreach' involves no extra meetings and has little to do with church premises. Downreach takes place anywhere and at any time. It is about allowing the Holy Spirit to deepen our everyday conversations. Often our chatting stays at the surface level, but sometimes layers peel off and we enter into a 'dialogue' in which the *logos* at the heart of every meeting reveals himself. This occurs more readily in conversations with strangers than with close friends.

Jesus' conversation with the Samaritan woman (4.4-26) is a good example of 'downreach'. Imagine Jesus sitting at the well. The woman has placed her water jar on the ground, stands and then finally sits, fascinated by this Jewish Rabbi. It is a conversation which transcends culture, religion, gender and social divide. The subject is 'water'. Jesus has nothing to draw with and the well is deep. The conversation echoes up and down the well. In a dialogue about 'living water' the woman follows Jesus as he takes her deep down into the recesses of her own being; her present discomfort, her current partner, memories of painful relationships, the thirst in her soul. The woman attempts to draw back by changing the subject. 'Let's talk about religion and church.' She knows that when the Messiah comes he will unveil all things. The man, who she describes as 'the one who told me all the things I ever did', says 'I AM'. It is a moment of profound illumination. Jesus has reached down into the deep well of the woman's experience and drawn up 'living water'.

John Drane gives a pertinent illustration of this in his reflections on the 'Dunblane Massacre'.[1] As he approached the gate of the school in which the killings had happened, he saw a gang of youths who took from their pockets 16 night-lights – one for each of the children who had been shot. They placed them in a circle, lit them, and then wondered what to do next. Spotting John Drane, who they identified as a minister, they called him and said, 'You'll know what to say.' With tears rolling down his face, he had no idea what to say or how to say it. His brief prayer, however, triggered something in the group:

> One said, 'What kind of world is this?'
> Another asked, 'Is there any hope?'
> Someone said, 'I wish I could trust God.'
> 'I'll need to change,' said a fourth one.

They were, reflects John Drane, reaching down into spiritual presence.

Thomas

The statement 'I am the way, and the truth, and the life' invites us to go on a journey with Jesus in which we move across and down beyond the box.

This statement comes in response to a specific question put by Thomas. Its application is particular rather than general. Thomas was so committed to following Jesus that he was prepared to 'die with him' (11.16). I do not think of him as a dull, dog-like disciple. He is a reflective person of perception, inquiry, understanding and courage. He, possibly more than the women, the 'beloved disciple' or Peter, is the writers' role model for discipleship. His following of Jesus is sacrificial, cross-centred and costly. Now he wants literally to touch the nail prints and thrust his fingers into the places of pain. We usually interpret this as his expression of doubt; we should rather interpret this as an exploration of our Lord's glorification. He wants to understand what following in 'the way' means. That's why questions come from his lips and why he is given a special resurrection appearance. Believing in Christ means copying the discipleship of Thomas. If we are to understand the full meaning of this journey into 'the way, and the truth, and the life' we too must put our hands into the fleshy wounds of the world; feel the pain and be present at the bleeding sores of humanity. Opting for some esoteric alternative, as some New Testament Christians did, is not an option.[2] The cross of suffering has to be embraced so that the tears of God can bring healing to the inhabitants of our planet.

There can be no deep discovery of the truth about God until one is physically in touch with the pain of others. Thomas may have seen the wounds of the crucified and dead Jesus. When the risen Christ comes and challenges him, it is to unfold this greater truth about the divine reality. John's Gospel reaches its climax as Thomas pushes confession beyond the box and cries, 'My Lord and my God' (20.28). He has found God to be so fully present in Jesus that his words erase all distinctions between the Father and

Son as well as between the physical and spiritual realities which have come to fruition in Jesus. Jesus confirms Thomas' faith but also pushes the limits back even further by celebrating those who believe without seeing (20.29).

Tradition has it that Thomas travelled to India and was martyred. He bequeathed in the traditions of the Mar Thoma Church a theology of the eternal *logos* and a legacy of worship which still evokes the mystery of resurrection.

Touching the void

I know nothing about mountain climbing but I have recently stumbled across a number of books by Joe Simpson and see a parallel between climbing and the ascent and descent of Christ. One of the earliest pictures of God in the Old Testament is associated with mountains, indeed the title 'El Shaddai' refers to a mountain-storm God. Joe Simpson's experience of the Eiger could equally be a description of an encounter with El Shaddai or the great I AM:

> I gazed at the Eiger. How would it change me? Past experiences had shaken me to the core, storms both real and metaphorical had raged through me, leaving an indelible sense of vulnerable fragility. Afterwards I was filled with a strength I had never experienced before, an exultant confidence born from standing unharmed within the tempest. I had lived through it. When the fear ebbed it was replaced with a mounting wonder at the beauty I had witnessed. The mountains were contradictory, in equal measure. I could remember their beauty yet could never fully recall the fear.[3]

Joe became famous because of his attempt to climb Siula Grande, a 6,356 metre remote peak in the Andes. A film has now been made of the book *Touching the Void*, describing this perilous adventure.[4] He and his fellow climber, Simon Yates, struggle with no back-up to the summit of this unclimbed mountain, only reaching the top by taking death-defying risks. Their moment of ecstasy is short-lived. Anticipating a quick descent they had used up all their fuel, an essential commodity for melting snow in these high dehydrating conditions. Their descent turned into a nightmare. Joe slips and breaks his leg. His chances of survival are minimal. Simon refuses to abandon him. He begins to lower Joe on a 150 feet rope down the 20,000 feet cliff face stopping again and again to unlash the rope, descend himself to where Joe clings in order to repeat the exercise. A raging storm drowns out Joe's agonizing screams of pain as his broken leg snarls and catches on the ice. As darkness falls Joe suddenly overshoots and is left dangling over the edge of a precipice. Simon cannot hold him. Beginning to slip, Simon can only save himself by cutting the rope. The ethics of his decision have been debated by mountain climbers ever since, though Joe maintains that he did the right thing, otherwise both would have been killed.

Joe fell. He plunged through the snow which broke his fall and disappeared down a crevasse. Somehow he managed to survive. Alone, poised on a narrow ledge over a bottomless pit, with a broken leg, no water, no rescue team and 20 miles from base camp he contemplates death. He cannot climb out. He is on his own without even the comfort of faith in God which he had abandoned years before. He will die like so many other climbers. His later book, *The Beckoning Silence*, is laced with references to mortality as he reflects on his own death and the deaths of so many of his former colleagues driven by their passion to scale the impossible. Joe is left with two choices: either to stay and die in agonizing pain or to lower himself deeper into the crevasse, entering a void in the vague hope that there might be a way out. That, he said, was the hardest decision he had ever taken in the whole of his life.

I cannot begin to contemplate his agonizing journey into the void and beyond. He, at the end of *Touching the Void*, says that his account of the terrible time in the crevasse and the crawl back to base camp totally fails to articulate just how dreadful were those solitary days of agony. 'I simply could not find words to express the sense of desolation.'

His adventure seems to reflect the strange language in John's Gospel about 'glorification' and 'being lifted up' which is really about descent into the crucifixion void. Here we have a journey which goes beyond package and pilgrimage. Why should we embark on such an adventure which touches the void? What lures us on? Joe Simpson seems to offer a profound insight into the Christian journey as the way to truth and life:

> I try simply to accept a spiritual sense of the world as life passes by. It is an overwhelming combination of all that I've experienced, felt, seen and cannot explain. It stays with me and refuses to depart, and it drives me again and again back to a place in which I am never certain; a place that is alluring because it will not be defined. It is intangible and must simply be lived. Perhaps that is why I loved mountains. They allowed me, however briefly, to escape, to act without the need to ask questions. I once read that for a mountaineer '... hardship and great effort hardly matters, since the life

of a mountain climber is an introduction to death, and when death comes or is about to come, the climber is at least partially satisfied'.[5]

Christians of 'the way, the truth, and the life' are drawn by this same beckoning silence, emanating from the great I AM. It stays with them. It will not depart. It lures them on. Yet, as a living and loving reality, it goes beyond what Simpson describes, for it both points to, and is the source of, 'abundant life'.

QUESTIONS

1. How far have you travelled beyond your own theological and cultural box? What have you discovered?

2. Share a recent conversation you have had in which you sensed you could have gone deeper but failed to do so. Without mentioning the name of the person, reassess the conversation. How could it have been different? What prevented you from a more significant 'downreach'?

3. Describe, if you are able, an occasion where your world was blown apart and you felt shattered and broken. What discoveries did you make of the truth about God?

PRAYER

Lord of all life,
I use thousands of words each day
  yet so few of them are about you.
I see and meet many people
    but I forget that in them I could be meeting
    you.
I busy myself in so much rushed activity
  that I blank out the silence within.
      Forgive me.
Help me to retune my life to the silent music of
  your beckoning presence.

Amen

9

Grace and truth

Let's remain open to God and keep moving on with him. There is life in abundance if we move beyond the box.

The previous chapter began by describing how I kept unpacking and repacking my case. I need to remind myself, especially as I have now sunk back into the clutches of Mammon, that I once discarded nearly all my belongings in little less than a month after arriving in Sri Lanka. When I travelled from Kandy to Buttula in the south my luggage consisted of malaria pills, water purifying tablets, a pencil, a knife, a notebook, soap, sponge, toothbrush, torch, a change of underwear, a little money and a passport together with the clothes I stood up in. I was learning to risk it and trust that God, who is full of grace and truth, would be there. I have learnt that life greets us beyond the box.

Abundant life

> I came that they may have life, and have
> it abundantly. I am the good shepherd.
> The good shepherd lays down his life for
> the sheep. (10.10-11)

Truth is found in the generosity of the God who invites us to participate in his abundant life. Grace and truth belong together (1.14). In John's Gospel we are invited to keep moving on from grace to grace. There is no stinginess within the trinitarian God and Father of our Lord Jesus Christ since 'From his fullness we have all received, grace upon grace' (1.16). Nathanael, who may well have been the 'beloved disciple', basking in the wonder of Jesus' revelation is informed that this was only the 'starters'.

Like Jacob of old (Genesis 28.10-22) he will see angels ascending and descending as they scale the impossible heights and depths of love (1.50-51).

In Nathanael's home town Jesus not only turns water into wine, he produces 120 gallons of the stuff; enough to float the guests on a shared exuberance of laughter and life. Unlike the measured manna of Moses, just enough for each day, Jesus whisks up a super-abundance of bread and fish. Even a crowd of thousands cannot consume it all so leftovers have to be collected in huge hampers. In the miracle story of John 21 the nets bulge with so many fish that the disciples are not able to haul them in. The prayer promises of Jesus are similarly beyond the box:

> Very truly, I tell you, the one who believes in me will also do the works that I do and, in fact, will do greater works than these, because I am going to the Father. I will do whatever you ask in my name, so that the Father may be glorified in the Son. (14.12-13)

It is too much to comprehend; for the men anyway. The women intuitively understand that grace cannot be measured, counted or controlled. Mary makes a reciprocal gesture as she lovingly lavishes her extravagant gift upon Jesus. The whole house is filled with the fragrance of love. Was she the same mysterious woman of 8.1-11 who experienced what it meant for the law of Moses to be superseded by the grace and truth of Jesus Christ? The contrast between miserly law and overflowing grace could not be more pronounced. The truth about life transcends our limiting boxes of theology and church. God is the God of resurrection life. His grace and truth cannot be contained. He leaps out of the theological cages in which we imprison him, for Jesus Christ is the I AM of God. As I stated at the start of this book, Mark's Gospel begins with John the Baptist; Matthew's with Abraham; Luke's with Adam; but John reaches back before time to the eternal cosmic Word. The writers of John's Gospel take us beyond the box into the very bosom of the Father. When they speak of 'the way, and the truth, and the life' they are not referring to a cosy theological construct but to the evolving, unfolding mystery of a living God who beckons us and draws us on. Sadly, grace and truth have often been understood as dogma and creed. The Holy Spirit has been tamed into church. Sacrificial discipleship has been reinvented as membership, the gospel dumbed down, worship domesticated and the Word reduced to ideas. Although *logos* is wisdom and conversation, it is also God's deed. For Christian disciples it is something to be enacted:

> If you love me, you will keep my commandments ... They who have my commandments and keep them are those who love me; and those who love me will be loved by my Father, and I will love them and reveal myself to them. (14.15, 21)

Beyond ourselves

In chapter 3 I described my own personal experience of being 'born again'. Looking back on that event with hindsight, I can see other significant incidents where God's grace was tangibly at work both before and after the decision made in the evangelist's tent. I could testify of how God, a few years before, revealed himself in a service of Holy Communion thereby stirring up my hunger for him. I could speak of how, in my late teens, God called me to become a Christian minister. I could recount how later he baptized me in the Holy Spirit. However, returning to the experience in the tent; from the moment I made the decision to open myself up to Christ I felt a peace and warmth within. The tingling feeling lasted some months. My converted friends were delighted with me and I basked in the glow of their approval. A Sunday school teacher reassured my troubled parents that 'Tom would grow out of it'. And so I did, but not in the way any of us expected. I grew out of the package in much the same manner as I grew out of the clothes I wore. I discovered Christianity was not simply a matter of signing up and getting the goods but rather of stepping onto an open road which went over the hills, down into valleys, sweeping onwards to some unseen destination. God was leading me on to discover the meaning of grace and truth.

Thirty-two years after leaving the evangelist's tent and struggling over the intervening time to follow in 'the way', my journal jumps forward to a further significant stage in my discipleship. I am on my way from Kandy to Buttula with the intention of visiting a tiny Christian community in a dangerous Buddhist heartland. It proved to be a roller-coaster ride of frustration, fear and wonder. At the end of this 24 hour trip I arrived feverish, tired and disorientated. I stepped out into a wilderness of burning heat. Not far from the roadside was a collection of huts. Had I come for this? I met Father Michael Rodrigo,[1] who has a particular dedication at the start of this book, and the two Salvatorian religious sisters. Later in the cool of the evening Sister Benedict took me around the village. We were followed everywhere by groups of local teenage lads, most of them drop-outs who hung around watching our every move. They had little money and no prospects. The drift into delinquency was easy. Many joined terrorist bands to become boy soldiers in Sri Lanka's brutal civil war.

The sun is sinking rapidly. The evening is a cool benediction after the burning heat of the day. Sister Benedict describes how the area once hosted seven gurgling streams which gushed through the forests bringing fertility to the soil, life for the peasant farmer, and renewal to a jungle vegetation rich in plants, butterflies and animal life. Following Independence, new colonizers arrived and, working through trans-national corporations, raped the forests, burnt trees and commandeered great tracks of land. Their systematic destruction of the environment robbed the village poor of their birds, beehives, deer and sambar on which they had relied for centuries. The resulting desertification had reduced the rainfall. What little water remained was diverted to the sugar estates. Yet grace and truth are to be found here. The poor Buddhist inhabitants greet me court-eously and welcome Sister Benedict with love. One of the local lads with a bicycle wants me to ride it. To his great delight I oblige. One lad sits on the cross bar and another hangs on at the back. I ride until we all fall off to the great amusement of those who gather to watch. They are astonished by my height and keep touching me. Little children gather round wanting to be picked up. Even the dogs seem to enjoy licking the mosquito repellent from my ankles. I become aware that I no longer feel ill.

As darkness descends, one of the lads leads me out into the jungle scrub to visit Chandrasare, a friend of his who, having fallen out with his family, has built a hut for himself away from the village. The visit of a lone white Englishman is a novelty in this dangerous place. Hospitality is offered. Although I feel uneasy I cannot refuse.

We sit on the ground in the small mud hut. There is no furniture, only large tins, rolled up blankets and a transistor radio without batteries. It is dark outside, the only sounds are noises from the forest and the ceaseless barking of dogs. The three of us sit on the hard earth while Chandrasare cooks rice and fish on a charcoal burner. The oil lamp fills the space with acrid smoke. At least it keeps the mosquitoes away. It is hot, sweaty and stuffy. There is only one plate. Chandrasare and Piyatilika watch me while I eat. There is pride on their faces. We are not able to speak one another's language. Piyatilika knows only one English word: 'happy'. He uses it again and again as a question. I shake my head in that strange Asian style which indicates 'yes'. They smile back. When I ask them they nod even more enthusiastically. The three of us sleep on the hard floor. I spent much of the night looking up at the stars through the gaps in the straw roof. The sense of the presence of God is palpable. I am more at peace with myself than I have been for a long time.[2]

It was only later next day I learnt that they had given me all the food they had. They had eaten nothing because they wished me to share the bounty of their gracious hospitality. In the sacrificial meal of these delinquent, non-Christian lads I had stumbled upon grace and abundant life. With few words the *logos* had become flesh in hospitality and food. A feeding in the wilderness had taken place. I now understand something of how those people who ate the loaves and fish (6.26) must have felt when Jesus worked his multiplication miracle.

The furthest shore

So the God of our journey keeps taking us beyond ourselves, for grace and truth transcend the limits of our expectation and comprehension. As Jesus told Nathanael at the very beginning: 'You will see greater things than these' (1.50). And he did. And so will we.

In the final chapter of the Gospel, Peter, Nathanael and some of the disciples go back to their old fishing job. There are mixed messages here. The reiterated challenge to Peter, 'Do you love me more than these', could suggest that Peter is still attached to his fishing boats (21.15-17). It could also be a reminder that he who promised to die with Jesus denied him. Equally the story may be a parable about the disciples engaging in a mission project seeking, as Peter was first commanded, to 'become fishers of men'. If so it was singularly unproductive. They needed the risen presence of Jesus to work the miracle of mission. Or again, the story may be a retake of Luke's account of the first calling of Peter beside the Sea of Galilee (Luke 5.1-11). Peter was told, 'Put out into the deep water and let down your nets for a catch.' There are many layers of meaning here.

As the new day dawns a cool breeze gently ripples the water. There is a stranger on the shore. They see him in the glow of the fire. He calls out to them, instructs them and through their obedience to his command all is revealed: an unbroken Church filled to capacity, life renewed, a fresh start. There is breakfast waiting for them, cooked on a charcoal burner. Not rice and fish, but bread and fish. They add their own offering to his meal of gracious hospitality. Then Jesus 'took the bread and gave it to them, and did the same with the fish' (21.13). This sharing is but a prelude to another stage of the journey. Their new adventure will take them to the 'furthest shore'. It will mean death by crucifixion for Peter and a peaceful end after a long life for the 'beloved disciple'. 'Come and see' (1.39) and the 'Follow me' (21.19) are the bookends of John's Gospel. But there is life outside the book. There is life far from the boats. There is abundant life beyond the box, for over the sea's horizon beyond death lies the 'furthest shore'.

Just before his death in 1991 Elliot Kendel, a former missionary in China, wrote a poem in which he looks back in reflection and forward in anticipation:

> The growing shadows mean a time of rest.
> The heat and passion of the day are gone.
> Yet sunset speaks of past and of tomorrow.
> There is some light within the darkness still.
>
> Times past hold moments of regret,
> Some things alas were best unsaid,
> Memories of some actions still remain.
> If only those ill-deeds had not been done
> And yet, they leave no heavy burden now;
> The end's in sight and they will be forgiven.
>
> If only one had earlier known the way,
> Or seen the chances that were there to take,
> One failed to match the glorious world around.
> We failed to reach the goodness of our friends,
> So much was not achieved or poorly done.

What now lives on? Not one's deeds and
    labours
But the flawed person that one was,
Yet that survives in hope because of love.
Love was the free gift of others, yet more
I also learned to love.
Such treasures must survive in human hearts
And in the very being of the world.[3]

Jesus said, 'I am the way, and the truth, and the life.'
    'Come, you will see.'
       'Follow me.'

QUESTIONS

1. Most churches carry on with programmes,
   activities, expectations and even theologies which
   are too heavy. What should your church stop
   doing? What personal baggage do you need to
   abandon?

2. Looking back over your own spiritual pilgrimage,
   how have you grown as a Christian? What have
   you learnt on the way? What must you now do in
   order to move on with God?

3. What have you learnt from the study of this book?
   What action does your church need to take to
   move on with God?

PRAYER

Lord Jesus Christ,
You are the way, the truth, and the life.
Grant that we may follow in your way,
so that we may discover your truth
and experience your life in all its fullness.

          Amen

Notes

1. Visiting the cathedral

1. Some smaller introductions and essays: Kenneth Grayston, *The Gospel of John*, Peterborough: Epworth Press, 1998. Raymond Brown, *The Community of the Beloved Disciple, The Life, Loves, and Hates of an Individual Church in New Testament Times*, New York: Paulist Press, 1979. David Catchpole, *Resurrection People: Studies in the Resurrection Narratives of the Gospels*, London: Darton, Longman & Todd, 2000, pp. 136-186.

   Some large books: Raymond Brown, *The Gospel according to John*, New York: Paulist Press, 1966. John Ashton, *Understanding the Fourth Gospel*, Oxford: Clarendon, 1993.

2. Tom Stuckey, *Into the Far Country, A Theology of Mission for an Age of Violence*, Peterborough: Epworth Press, 2003.

3. The idea of these six sections come from the following texts (2.1-11, 5.1-9, 6.1-14, 7.6-14, 9.1-7, 11.1-44).

4. 4.26, 6.35, 8.12, 10.7, 10.14, 11.25, 14.6, 15.1, 18.5.

5. 13.23, 19.26, 20.2, 21.7, 21.22-24.

2. Shrines and vines

1. Pete Ward, *Liquid Church*, Carlisle: Paternoster Press, 2002.

2. Stuckey, *Into the Far Country*, pp.129-130.

3. The breaking of the waters

1. Frank Lake, *Clinical Theology*, London: Darton, Longman & Todd, 1966. Frank Lake, *Tight corners in pastoral counselling*, London: Darton, Longman & Todd, 1981.

2. Jean Vanier, *Drawn into the Mystery of Jesus through the Gospel of John*, London: Darton, Longman & Todd, 2004, p. 108.

3. Personal Journal.

4. Broken churches

1. John Macquarrie, *Christian Unity and Christian Diversity*, London: SCM Press, 1975, pp. 17-19.

5. Martha's keys?

1. Edwina Gateley, *A Warm Moist Salty God, Women journeying towards wisdom*, Wheathampstead: Anthony Clarke, 1994, pp. 38-40.

2. Mary Grey, *Redeeming the Dream, Feminism, Redemption and Christian Tradition*, London: SPCK, 1993, pp. 42-43.

3. This is a constant theme which keeps reappearing throughout *Into the Far Country* as I explore God's mission from the perspective of Covenant.

4. Mary Grey, *The Wisdom of Fools? Seeking Revelation for Today*, London: SPCK, 1995, pp. 22-28, pp. 49-55.

5. Edwina Gateley, *I hear a seed growing*, Wheathampstead; Anthony Clarke, 1990, pp. 264-265.

6. Crazy people

1. Merfyn Temple, *My Three Days in Mugabe's Hell Hole*, Devon: Speed Print, 2003.

2. Nelson Mandela, *Long Walk to Freedom*, London: Abacus, 1996, pp. 273f.

3. A.E. Harvey, *Jesus on Trial: A Study in the Fourth Gospel*, London: SPCK, 1976, p. 46f.

4. Brian Keenan, *An Evil Cradling*, London: Vintage, 1992, p. 99.

5. Ken Kelsey, *One Flew Over the Cuckoo's Nest*, London: Picador, 1973, p. 61.

6. John Bunyan, *The Pilgrim's Progress*, London: Collins, 1953, p. 104.

7. Passion and petition

1. Trevor Dennis, *Imagining God*, London: SPCK, 2001, pp. 11-14.

2. Stuckey, *Into the Far Country*, pp. 44-47.

3. G.A. Studdert Kennedy, *The Unutterable Beauty*, London: Hodder and Stoughton, 1957, p. 132.

4. No 685, *Hymns & Psalms*, London: Methodist Publishing House, 1983.

5. Jean Vanier, *Drawn into the Mystery of Jesus Through the Gospel of John,* p. 280-28.

6. The concluding prayer is by Peter Millar, Iona Community, from a prayer first published in *An Iona Prayer Book*, Canterbury Press.

8. The beckoning silence

1. John Drane's story found in Michael Riddell, *Threshold of the Future*, London: SPCK, 1997, pp. 30f.

2. At the beginning of chapter 4, I referred to the three New Testament letters attributed to John. It appears that the breakaway Christians addressed here had so emphasized the spirit of Jesus that they attached little significance to his physical humanity.

3. Joe Simpson, *The Beckoning Silence*, London: Vintage, 2003, p. 159.

4. Joe Simpson, *Touching the Void*, London: Vintage, 1997.

5. Joe Simpson, *The Beckoning Silence,* p. 114-115.

9. Grace and truth

1. More information about Father Michael Rodrigo, his theology, life and death can be found in my book, *Into the Far Country*, pp. 61-68, 148-150.

2. Personal Journal.

3. Poem given to me by his sister, Lenice Bailey.